SUNRACING

by

Richard and Melissa King
with contributions by J. Ward Phillips

HRD
Human Resource Development Press
Amherst, Massachusetts

Foreword

I can still remember when my dad went to that photovoltaic conference out in Las Vegas in September 1988. When he came back he began to tell my mom about solar cars and how they worked.

I asked, "What are solar cars?"

My mom answered, "Solar cars run on the sun." But I wanted a better answer.

And I got one. In June 1989 my dad was gone for one week. My mom had said he was going to see a solar car race.

I asked her again, "What are solar cars?" hoping to get a better explanation this time. I did.

"Solar cars run on the sun," she said. "Solar panels collect the sun's rays and turn them into electricity without polluting the environment."

"Wow!" I said.

In July 1990 my dad went to another solar car race. He went to the GM SUNRAYCE USA. By this time I knew what solar cars were. I was excited, not puzzled. I waited anxiously for his calls about the race every night.

In November 1990 my dad went to the World Solar Challenge in Australia. I was again excited. Although he didn't call every night, when he did I was always full of questions.

And when my dad and mom wrote this book I was more than happy. The world was finally going to know about solar cars and about how they can change our future.

by Bryan M. King

age 9

SUNRACING

by Richard and Melissa King
with contributions by J. Ward Phillips

Photography: Richard King

Design and Production: Beth L. Brennan

Contributing Photos:
Maureen Williams; Kevin Treynor; Gene Smith; Art Boyt;
Urs Muntwyler; Paul MacCready; Hans Tholstrup; Mike Shelton;
Susan Fancy; Ed Clarke; Bob Francis

Acknowledgements:
We wish to thank J. Ward Phillips for his continuous support and encouragement. Without him the book would never have gotten off the ground. Special thanks to Hans Tholstrup, Urs Muntwyler, Paul MacCready and James Worden who gave time to be interviewed while we conducted our research. There were also many individuals who sent us information, video footage and photos we wish to thank: Susan Fancy, Art Boyt, Mike and Tina Shelton, Ed Clarke, Maureen Williams, Erik Thatcher, Michael Seal, David Holloway, Paula Finnegan, Kevin Treynor, Gene Smith, and the solar car teams from Clarkson, Drexel, Western Washington, California State LA, Waterloo, Ottawa, Puerto Rico, RIT and others too numerous to note. Finally, the book would not have been possible without the many people involved in building, racing, and sponsoring the solar powered cars. To these individuals with "can-do" attitudes, we thank you for making the adventure come alive.

Copyright © 1993 by Richard King

Human Resource Development Press, Inc., Publishers
22 Amherst Road, Amherst, Massachusetts 01002-9709
(413) 253-3488 (Massachusetts)
1-800-822-2801 (outside Massachusetts)

Printed in the United States of America.

First Edition, First Printing, October, 1993

Library of Congress Cataloging in Publication Data

ISBN 0-87425-227-X

Table of Contents

GM SUNRAYCE USA began at the EPCOT Center in Orlando, Florida on July 9, 1990. With EPCOT's Spaceship Earth glistening in the background, 32 solar car teams readied themselves for the 11-day, 1,644-mile race to Detroit, Michigan. In the foreground is the University of Maryland's "Pride of Maryland." The University of Michigan's "Sunrunner" is in the background.

Introduction

The early morning sunshine bestowed its blessing upon a crowd of curious spectators as 32 futuristic-looking solar-powered vehicles slid silently into position. To the sound of enthusiastic cheers, each solar car moved into place under the azure blue sky. The cars were all different shapes and sizes; some like horizontal teardrops, some like winged torpedoes with wheels, and some like small spaceships designed for land mobility. Could there really be drivers inside? What was their mission?

Intrigued by the magic of the moment, hundreds of people looked on as the sleek, streamlined vehicles soaked up the sun's rays. EPCOT Center's Spaceship Earth sparkled in the background in apparent approval. The solar cells which adorned the car bodies made it possible for the vehicles to fuel up with sunlight. Their rounded and angular surfaces glistened as the cells dutifully captured the sun's energy. In a brief flirtation with tomorrow's automotive technology, 32 solar electric cars were at the starting line for GM SUNRAYCE USA, ready to "race for the future."

That was the scene on July 9, 1990, just before the largest North American solar car race was about to begin. The first electric car was built in 1838, but no one imagined that some day electric cars might be charged by the sun's rays. Whoever would have dreamed that we would be cruising along at highway speeds on sunpower? Ironically, Charles Fritts and Edmond Becquerel's seminal work in photovoltaics (solar electricity) occurred only one year later, in 1839. They discovered that an electric current was produced when light struck a selenium panel. Like many scientific discoveries, these two, the electric car and the photo-electric effect, occurred separately. But what could have been a dramatic opportunity for collaboration resulted in distinctly divergent paths. The possible link between electric cars and photovoltaics was not recognized for nearly 150 years.

The "Star II" solar car built by Crowder College is inched up to the starting line in the EPCOT parking lot.

At the turn of the century there were more electric cars on the road than gasoline powered cars. Electric cars were very popular because of their easy starting compared to hand cranking an early gas engine.

In the early 1900's, electric cars were quite a common sight. At that time, the internal combustion engine was regarded as dirty, noisy, and fairly unreliable. In fact, 38 percent of all privately-owned cars in the U.S. were electric vehicles at the turn of the century.

Electric-powered taxis, milk trucks, and trolley cars were a common sight up through the 1930's. But the limited range of battery charges, coupled with unavailable electric power sources outside city boundaries, seemed to seal the fate of these early electric automobiles. They were destined to become museum artifacts.

With marked improvements in the internal combustion engine (ICE) and the increased distance it promised drivers with quick fill-ups at the gas pumps, electric cars faced unbeatable odds. In an ironic twist of fate, it was the invention of the electric starter motor which contributed to the success of the ICE and the demise of electric automobiles. Earlier cars with ICEs had to be hand-cranked, a challenging task for even the strongest individuals. The electric starter eliminated this troublesome step, making it possible for almost anyone to "get up and go" in a gasoline-powered auto. The convenience of the ICE was a powerful marketing tool.

From the 1940's to the 1970's, electric vehicles were more often seen at museum exhibitions than on the road. At that time, oil supplies were plentiful. Many Americans believed that "bigger was better" when it came time to consider new car purchases.

This is a typical scene in cities throughout the world as millions of people take to the highways each day. Automobiles are responsible for over a third of all air pollution, a direct result of burning billions of gallons of gasoline each and every day.

American car manufacturers produced thousands of gasoline-powered chariots for a travel-conscious public. People were mighty thankful for the freedom granted by these automotive wonders. Before long the nation-on-wheels had instituted drive-in banking,

In sunracing (competing in a solar car race), the object is to collect as much solar energy as possible in order to drive the fastest and go the farthest on a tankful of sunshine. The sport of solar racing is full of challenge and excitement as teams try to outdistance each

In a side-by-side comparison of automobile technologies in similar stages of development, Virginia Tech (left) and Cal State L.A. (right) raced their cars against a 1931 Model "A" Ford and narrowly won. Given another 60 years of development, one wonders how much better a solar car would fare against today's automobiles.

drive-in restaurants, and drive-in movie theaters. And so began a long-term love affair with the automobile.

During that thirty-year period, economic growth in the United States sped forward at lightning's pace. Any real concerns about the earth's dwindling resources went unheeded, as did environmentalists' worries about the state of the biosphere. Then, without warning, the oil crisis of the seventies created havoc with contemporary views of our energy future. Suddenly, both scientists and politicians saw their perspectives turned upside down as leaders the world over scrambled to search for solutions.

Today the electric vehicle is considered a possible solution. With no tailpipe emissions, the electric vehicle is a clean alternative to the ICE. A solar electric vehicle goes one step further by relying upon renewable solar energy for its power.

A solar race car is a specially-designed lightweight electric vehicle. Unbelievable as it may seem, the average 400-pound (250 kg) solar race car equipped with an electric motor and batteries travels from place to place on 1,200 watts of power...about the same as a portable hair dryer! And how does it refuel? On sunshine. Its solar cells, solid state devices that convert sunlight directly into electricity, provide the power to charge the batteries and move the car.

other while contending with changing weather conditions. Sunracing becomes a learning experience for all involved.

Beyond its application to power automobiles, photovoltaics (solar electricity) has tremendous potential for helping meet today's energy needs. Although the photo-electric effect was discovered in 1839, the first practical working solar cells were not fabricated until 1954. Early solar cells were very expensive, and were used mainly to provide electricity for space satellites. Now, with improved technology and reduced cost, solar cells are more practical for everyday use. This makes photovoltaics a realistic alternative to fossil fuels as a source of energy today.

As we approach the 21st century, there are critical decisions to be made regarding our energy future. Will we choose a brighter path for tomorrow's generations? Or will we continue to rely on nonrenewable energy sources which pollute our environment? And what role does the sport of solar car racing play?

Welcome aboard our sunracing journey. In this book you will find out about the dawn of a new sport and what makes it so significant. As you read about the pioneers who are pushing technology forward, we hope you will be inspired.

Solar cars

Solar cars blend bicycle technology with airplane technology as they strive to be as lightweight and aerodynamic as possible. The results produce unique and innovative designs.

Some solar cars weigh as little as 300 pounds, but most average 500 to 600 pounds. They need to be light because their motors are sized to run most efficiently at two horsepower. The solar arrays that they carry generate about one kilowatt of electricity on a continuous basis, or about one horsepower. Another kilowatt, or horsepower, is gained from batteries which they keep charged with the solar array. It is impressive to watch these cars cross continents in as few as five days.

Sunracing requires skill and strategy. The challenge is to design a car that can collect the most sunlight and use it the most efficiently so it can drive the fastest. Since the car is dependent on sunlight, it is important to constantly update strategy based on the weather up ahead. But weather predictions are rarely exact, so there is a sense of unpredictability that adds excitement to the race.

The winner of the 1989 Swiss Tour de Sol.

Above: *GM's "Sunraycer" won the 1987 World Solar Challenge in Australia.*

Left: *Professors of engineering from the Engineering University of Biel in Switzerland led a team in designing and building this solar race car to compete in the 1990 World Solar Challenge.*

I. Sunracing: A Tale of Adventurism and Scientific Ingenuity

One aspect of natural history which continually repeats itself is that change, if left on its own, takes time. In the grand scheme of our planet, evolutionary change rather than revolutionary change predominates. Adaptations for survival among species of plants and animals proceed gradually, with Mother Nature oblivious to the demands of any intrusive time structure.

But humans DO have the unique capacity to impose their will on the natural order of things to create new ways of coping with their surroundings. Indeed, successful leadership in a human community is often marked by the influence of those who refuse to be dominated, so that they themselves might become the dominant forces of change.

In fact, many individuals in the forefront of change inspire us as leaders....the visionaries who dare to challenge the status quo. Who were the bold entrepreneurs determined to make a difference in our plans for an energy-bright future? Why did they choose "the road not taken" in

pursuit of their dreams for change?

Hans Tholstrup emerged as one of those individuals with a keen sense of realism. A man of ceaseless energy, Tholstrup has long been committed to an activist approach to the energy crisis. Not content to sit back while others brainstormed possible solutions to any problem, Tholstrup insisted upon setting examples. Endowed with a knack for ingenuity and a real craving for breathtaking adventures, he decided to "force technology forward." He could not wait to see what happened. Tholstrup was impatient with the reluctance of industry to initiate change and was anxious to explore new alternatives for a future full of energy.

Born in Denmark in 1944, Hans Tholstrup seemed destined to display his Viking heritage by embarking upon adventures to conquer

Hans Tholstrup (above, left) with members of an Hawaiian solar car team in Switzerland during the 1991 Tour de Sol.

The University of Michigan's "Sunrunner" stands ready to race in the 1990 GM SUNRAYCE USA.

brave new worlds. His quest for the new and unusual began when he was a young boy. He enjoyed exploring, was fascinated by movement, and was often found traveling "somewhere" on his bicycle or moped.

Tholstrup also liked to take things apart to see just how they worked. After all, he reasoned, if someone had put it together, some-

Hans Tholstrup was the first person to build a solar powered car. In 1982 he drove his solar powered car, called the "Quiet Achiever," over 2500 miles from Perth to Sidney, Australia. In 1984 he had the inspiration to create a race to help push the technology forward. He named it the World Solar Challenge, and in 1987, 35 vehicles from around the world competed in this historic event. Here he ponders his next race.

one else could dismantle and reassemble it in a better way.

Books were also an inspiration and exciting diversion for young Tholstrup. Stories about Kon Tiki, Robinsoe Crusoe, and Tarzan were among his favorites. He was also fond of books about racing car drivers and pilots. Unbeknownst to him then, his own future exploits would rival those thrilling tales of adventure.

Competitive by nature and fueled by optimism, Tholstrup thrived on the challenge of proving he could do what had not been done before. After finishing high school, he decided to go to Australia. But he had no means of getting there. Undaunted and determined, 18-year-old Tholstrup hitched a ride on a steamer, arriving three months later, not much older but much more "seasoned" as a traveler.

An uncanny expert at devising ways to attract attention, Tholstrup found adventure with race car driving, boating, and flying. In

1969, he became the first person to circumnavigate Australia in a 16-foot open boat. He was also the first person to drive across the continent in a 4-wheel drive truck. Then, in his quest to prove he could do what others had not done before, a bold young Tholstrup completed a motorcycle trip around the world in 27 days.

Taking to the air, Tholstrup figured he had to set another record with wings. He bought a small plane, got his pilot's license in ten days, and made a solo flight around the world in just three months.

While these amazing feats kept Tholstrup busy, they were not quite enough to fuel his active mind. He did some studying to learn more about energy. Realizing the limitations of nonrenewable energy supplies, Tholstrup was convinced the world should consider alternative energy sources to solve the energy crisis. But how to convince the rest of the world? He needed another attention-getter, an avenue into the spotlight.

In Australia, Tholstrup had driven in car economy runs, attempting to eke out the most mileage per gallon in competitive events. He was intrigued by the idea of figuring out how FAR a car could go, instead of how FAST it could go. Although these races did prove the value of efficiency, he believed commercial travel would have a more significant effect on prices and inflation, since trucks are the vehicles that carry so many of the goods and necessities on to consumers.

In 1978, Tholstrup initiated the world's first economy run for commercial vehicles. The race included 10-wheelers, small delivery trucks, and every kind of transport vehicle imaginable. To weigh the trucks down, Tholstrup loaded them with canned goods, which they then carried from Melbourne to Sydney in the economy run. The race proved that drivers could save at least 30 percent in fuel expenditure.

Although convinced that energy conservation was a must, it was learning about solar cell technology that catapulted Tholstrup's enthusiasm in new directions. Amazed that these wafer-thin photovoltaic cells could convert sunlight directly into electricity, he saw a possible application for transportation needs. Why not utilize the sun's vast energy output to power terrestrial vehicles? Over and over again he was told, "It cannot be done." Ironically, it was this response that motivated Tholstrup even more. He set out to prove that it COULD be done, despite all the grim predictions of impossibility.

In 1981 Tholstrup read about the flight of Paul MacCready's Solar Challenger across the

English Channel. Powered only by sunlight, this achievement ignited sparks of imagination in Tholstrup's mind. Wow! Flying on solar power. What a great idea! If someone could fly with it, then he could drive with it.

Just one year later Tholstrup maneuvered the idea of a solar-powered land vehicle from concept to reality. With fellow Australian Larry Perkins, an engineer and accomplished race car driver, Tholstrup designed and built a solar car for $12,000.

The world's first Solar Trek, sponsored by British Petroleum of Australia, proved that this crazy dream of driving on a tank filled with sunshine was serious stuff. Tholstrup and Perkins were determined to beat the 1912 record set by Francis Birtles. Birtles is credited with the first motor vehicle crossing of Australia, accomplished in 28 days.

Called the "Quiet Achiever," Tholstrup's solar car weighed 125 kilograms (276 pounds) and consisted of a tubular steel frame, four bicycle tires, batteries, and an electric motor. Actually, it looked more like an oversized bathtub on wheels than a car. Gracing the top of this vehicle were 20 solar panels which formed a horizontal roof. Equipped with two 12-volt batteries and two simple power switches, the Quiet Achiever could travel up to 25 mph (40 kph) on solar electricity.

The car's chassis could be lifted out of the body quite easily for any necessary repairs, and the entire car could be reassembled in five minutes. With surprising reliability, the car never broke down once during their long and arduous journey.

The trip began in Perth, on the western coast of Australia, on December 19, 1982. Intentionally, the trip's beginning coincided with the summer solstice in the southern hemisphere. Averaging 11 hours of travel per day, the dynamic racing duo evoked curious stares all along the 2,519-mile (4,052-kilometer) route. Enduring temperatures of near 50 degrees Celsius (122 degrees Fahrenheit) across the Nullarbor Plain, the car performed well despite frequent gusty winds and very rough roads.

Tholstrup and Perkins discovered they had underestimated the car's power. Even the steep grades of the Victoria Pass in the Great Dividing Range did not stop this Achiever from achieving. And never before had Tholstrup seen such support from the public. He felt as if the "whole world had burst into a smile."

On January 7, 1983, Tholstrup's Quiet Achiever reached the Sydney Opera House, completing its cross-continental race in 20 days. It beat Birtles' record by eight days and thrilled the 2,000 spectators as it came racing into Sydney.

Engineers were shocked by the successful maiden voyage of this chariot of the sun. How could an "amateur" have designed and built this unique earthcraft? How could this first of its kind vehicle have made it all the way across the harsh Australian Outback without resorting to conventional gasoline power? The Minister

This is the first solar powered car ever built. It was designed and built by Hans Tholstrup and Larry Perkins in 1982. Called the "Quiet Achiever," they drove it across the Australian continent in 20 days using only sunlight for power.

for National Development and Energy poured a flask of Indian Ocean water (carried from Perth) into the Pacific Ocean. This symbolic gesture showed that two oceans had been linked by solar power and human ingenuity.

During his epic adventure in the Quiet Achiever, Tholstrup became convinced that "a new era was beginning." As he considered how to promote research on solar car technology, he created the "brain sport." He would initiate a solar car racing event, encouraging scientists and engineers to work together in preparation for a competitive road rally. The reward would be honor rather than profit, the honor that comes with developing something slightly ahead of its time; something that would ultimately be valuable to the world.

And so the World Solar Challenge was born. Tholstrup formulated the rules for the solar car competition and put together a comprehensive set of regulations. He wrote specifications for the dimensions of the vehicles, size of the solar arrays, ballasted weight of each driver, and all necessary safety features.

Tholstrup also prescribed the daily schedule for racing. Running time would commence at 8 AM and end at 5 PM. Charging time was restricted to two-hour periods before and after each day's driving hours. Batteries could be charged only from solar panels on the cars.

To ensure compliance with these rules, Tholstrup planned for official observers to travel behind each competitor. Observers were to remain in sight of their assigned solar cars at all times, carefully recording race-related activities in a log-book. Should there be any question about any car's performance, observers would have adequate documentation.

Who should be contacted about the World Solar Challenge? How could potential racers from all over the globe be reached? Tholstrup set the process in motion with limited financial support from a few sponsors but without any direct technical assistance.

In a race against all odds, Tholstrup made his vision a reality. He sent out official announcements to everyone he could think of. One by one, the responses came back to his office on Bribie Island. Race entrants were from Australia, the United States, Japan, Denmark, Switzerland, Pakistan, and West Germany. The World Solar Challenge was off and running.

This is the official program for the 1987 World Solar Challenge. It contained route information and pictures of the entrants participating in the first solar car race across Australia.

During Tholstrup's epic journey in the Quiet Achiever he had to travel through some of the continent's harshest interior deserts. As this photo of the North-South railroad depicts, the hot arid country seems to extend on forever.

One of Tholstrup's invitations landed on Roger Smith's desk in December 1986. Then Chairman of General Motors, Smith had never heard of Hans Tholstrup, but he took time to read over the regulations for the solar car race. He was interested enough to take action. Smith passed the package on to Howard Wilson, then vice president of Hughes Aircraft Company, a subsidiary of GM- Hughes Electronics.

An electrical engineer vested with joint control of projects with GM, Wilson was a forward-looking individual. Ever on the lookout for ways to demonstrate the talents of both companies, he was intrigued by Tholstrup's announcement of the race. The opportunity for technological innovation in an international competition might lead to unprecedented results.

Above: The General Motors solar car and team that won the first World Solar Challenge. Their car, called the "Sunraycer," finished two days ahead of its nearest competitor and set a record that still stands today.

Left: Howard Wilson was the project leader for the General Motors/ Hughes Aircraft/Aerovironment corporate team that designed and built the Sunraycer.

Wilson decided that a GM-Hughes entry in the World Solar Challenge was a great idea. The timing was right. GM had the expertise in automotive design, electric motors, mechanical components, and reliability testing. Hughes had experience with photovoltaic cells, solar arrays, and lightweight batteries. Together, he reasoned, they could develop a solar-powered car to beat the competition under Australia's blazing sun.

Wilson sought out Paul MacCready to help him design the solar car. For Paul MacCready, interest in the World Solar Challenge was a natural extension of his tinkerings with efficiency in motion. Never content to accept "what is," this mastermind of aerodynamic engineering was well-known for tackling "what can be." When contacted by his former classmate from the California Institute of Technology about collaboration with GM-Hughes on a solar-powered car, MacCready's instinct was to accept the challenge.

When MacCready read the information about the World Solar Challenge in February 1987, he had no idea what vehicle design might be best. He DID know that a winning strategy depended upon trade-offs between power and aerodynamics. He DID sense that his involvement might make a difference. Intuitively, he felt this project could make an impact upon

transportation planning for the 21st century.

An unassuming, introspective man, MacCready's calm, quiet demeanor puts others at ease immediately. But hidden beneath this restful exterior is the workings of a highly active scientific mind. In his presence, one can almost sense his constant wonderings. His quest to learn seems an infinite voyage. At the same time, he has an uncanny ability to carefully sort out and organize what he learns.

One wonders where MacCready's philosophical commitment to "energy minimalism" comes from. Why is he inclined to suggest that we can "do more with less?" Why does he insist on pushing technology forward to unexpected boundaries? Was it his belief in the power of competition, his fascination with putting things together in ways no one had ever thought pos-

Dr. Paul MacCready (center) at the 1990 GM SUN-RAYCE USA Victory Dinner.

9

sible, or an instinctual desire to conserve Mother Nature's precious resources?

Even in his childhood, MacCready took to flights of imagination. A model airplane enthusiast, he spent countless hours as a young boy building model airplanes. His interest in ultralight aircraft began at an early age. Balsa wood models which flew so quietly and freely captured his fancy. Mimicking birds in flight, his experience fashioning these winged gliders set the stage for later achievements with his human-powered aircraft.

But young MacCready did not build only the usual airplane models. He designed ornithopters (with flapping wings), gyroplanes (with both vertical and horizontal propellers), and other rather strange-looking aeronautic craft. In 1939, at age 14, he had set his first world flight record with one of his own aircraft. For MacCready, experimenting with new ideas was a very powerful motivator. If he could figure out a new approach to an old problem or demonstrate an entirely new principle, he would be satisfied. He seemed driven to go beyond established boundaries. The skies above were a fitting destination for this individual who was so determined to reach new heights.

If you visit the National Air and Space Museum in Washington, D.C., you will see an example of MacCready's genius on display. His Gossamer Condor, the 70-pound (32-kg) flying machine with the 96-foot (29-meter) wingspan, occupies a place of honor beside Charles Lindbergh's Spirit of St. Louis.

MacCready knew that the coveted Kremer Prize, established by British industrialist Henry Kremer in 1959, had gone unclaimed for 18 years. The prize was to be awarded for the first sustained human-powered flight (one mile in length) over a figure-eight course. In the early seventies, MacCready was sure it could be done, and he was sure that he could design an aircraft to do it.

After a year-long odyssey of experimentation and frequent disappointment, the high-powered development crew of the Gossamer Condor tasted success. In August 1977, MacCready's awkward-looking aircraft with the bicyclist at the helm made its debut with official Kremer observers. The Gossamer Condor flew for seven-and-a-half minutes, traveling 1.35 miles (2.2 kilometers) on pedal power alone at Shafter Airport near Bakersfield, California. Sustained human-powered flight was now more than a theoretical possibility.

The astonishing triumph of the Gossamer Condor, piloted by Bryan Allen, created an indelible link between Paul MacCready's name and aviation history. Suddenly, journalists from all over the world wanted the story. His dedicated persistence and firm belief in what was "doable" resulted in sudden celebrity status in the scientific community.

That accomplishment may have been the true beginning of MacCready's crusade for efficiency. The Condor project made him acutely aware of the delicate balance between technology and the environment. Human-powered flight was not a contest but a delicate balance between the raw forces of nature and human ingenuity. This point of view has been a consistent trademark of many of MacCready's projects and led to his classic label as an "energy minimalist."

The Gossamer Condor's success stimulated the development of a second human-powered aircraft, the Gossamer Albatross. MacCready and his team were after another Kremer Prize, this one to cross the English Channel. In 1979, the Albatross and its pilot, Bryan Allen, surprised the world by flying from England to France on raw muscle and sheer endurance against all odds. As the Albatross touched down after two hours and 49 minutes of human-powered flight, aeronautical history had to be rewritten once again.

Two years later, in 1981, an even more symbolic feat made the news. MacCready's solar-powered airplane, the Solar Challenger, flew the 163 miles (262 km) from Paris to England on sunshine fuel. But this time, MacCready was not after a prize. This time, he wanted to demonstrate a relatively new technology: photovoltaics. With the Solar Challenger, MacCready pursued a new objective. Could he set a new record and boost interest in alternative energy at the same time? He thought so.

The 16,128 solar cells mounted on the Challenger's wings and fuselage were left over from a NASA satellite project. They delivered 3,000 watts of power, operating at 13 percent efficiency. The aircraft was also equipped with a 2.75 horsepower motor. MacCready's Solar Challenger achieved what seemed more magical than believable. Its top speed was measured at 47 mph (76 kph) and soared to heights of 11,000 feet (335 meters).

This incredible 217-pound (98 kg) flying machine was constructed of a unique combination of durable, lightweight materials which proved to be reliably strong in flight. In five hours and 23 minutes, the Solar Challenger demonstrated that by stretching the limits of technology, humans can make quantum leaps.

In 1981 Dr. Paul MacCready designed, built and successfully flew his solar powered airplane across the English Channel. Called the "Solar Challenger," it crossed the 163-mile channel in five hours and 23 minutes.

It was powered by 3,000 watts of solar cells and had a top speed of 47 mph. This stunning achievement was the key inspiration which led to the creation of the sport of solar car racing.

Recognizing that solar power is not a realistic alternative for everyday flying, MacCready says this project was more "a symbol and a stimulus." If he could focus more attention on solar energy, then maybe he would help push the technology forward. As it turns out, his 1981 accomplishment with solar-powered flight did make a difference.

Unbeknownst to MacCready, news of the Solar Challenger was the key inspiration for Hans Tholstrup, two oceans away. After reading an article about MacCready's solar airplane, the bold Australian adventurer decided to build his own solar vehicle. If someone else could fly on sunpower, then he could drive on it. Tholstrup's solar-powered Quiet Achiever was an offspring of MacCready's Solar Challenger. And so it is that one historical event led to the birth of another, sparked by the ever-ingenious human spirit.

The solar car line-up minutes before the start of Day Three of the 1989 Swiss Tour de Sol.

II. The Sunracing Spirit Catches On

On a third continent, the plans of yet another young scientist were brewing. A 26-year-old Swiss electronics engineer named Urs Muntwyler was seeking a way to educate the public about the benefits and potential of solar electric power. During a late-night brainstorming session with some friends in September 1984, Muntwyler had an idea. At the time, the idea seemed both radical and brilliant. But he held to his conviction that a race of solar-powered vehicles could raise public awareness of photovoltaics.

A calm, collected individual with a lion's share of Swiss precision and orderliness, Muntwyler is an electrician by trade. Like many others, he aspired to soar "on the wing" as a teenager. He got his pilot's license before he learned to drive a car. Gliders and sailplanes captured his fancy more than mechanical flights, and he spent hours aloft in the skies over Switzerland's majestic mountain ranges.

Muntwyler knew of Paul MacCready's accomplishments and was inspired by his aerodynamic wizardry. In fact, he had made use of MacCready's calculations and sailplane models

Urs Muntwyler at work directing the Swiss Tour de Sol.

on several occasions. After the Solar Challenger made its successful flight over the English Channel, Muntwyler poured over the articles about this unique solar aircraft. He credits MacCready's influence, claiming that it made a substantial impact on his own thinking and achievements.

While working for a small photovoltaics (PV) firm in Switzerland, Muntwyler was directed to help the marketing department increase the company's visibility. At first, he thought a large demonstration of photovoltaic power might be the answer. But he realized the limits of having a stationary display. Next, he wondered if they could load a PV system onto a trailer and drive it around to show people. The more he thought about it, a parade seemed a great idea. Solar electric cars could drive through towns, attracting attention while showing that solar energy actually powered the motors in the cars. But he wanted something more exciting to attract the attention of the public. Then, he came up with the idea for a competitive race of solar-powered cars. That inspiration turned out to be right on target. The Tour de Sol was born.

Muntwyler worked with two other solar experts, Josef Jenni and Markus Heimlicher. They prepared a comprehensive set of regulations for the Tour de Sol, an international road rally for solar electric vehicles. In November 1984, they issued the first official announcement for the race. They spread the word in newspapers and on television. Five months later, they were shocked to have had more than 70 responses from all over Europe. The world's first solar car competition was off to a great start. What began as a far-fetched idea became a viable entity.

Propelled by a desire to share technology's startling advances with an ever-inquisitive public, Muntwyler and his colleagues initiated their version of the "race for the future."

Once the public relations campaign for the Tour de Sol was in high gear, people from all over called Muntwyler to ask, "Where can we buy a solar car?" or "How do we build

one?" He was pleasantly surprised and more motivated than ever. Four months before the race, Muntwyler and his wife, Sigrid, organized a conference called "The Technology of Solar Cars." This was an attempt to galvanize support for their event and to provide useful information to would-be competitors.

On June 23, 1985, there were 58 cars registered at the Tour de Sol starting line near Winterthur, Switzerland. The competitors were an eclectic mix of individuals and companies, including an engineering school, an inventive farmer, and Mercedes-Benz. Much to their surprise, the drivers discovered a receptive public all along the race route. Traveling on secondary roads in Switzerland, these vehicles were a moving public display of solar technology.

1985 Tour de Sol

The first Swiss Tour de Sol was held on June 23, 1985 near Winterthur, Switzerland. With no prior experience and less than eight months to build their solar cars, 58 teams showed up for the event.

The first Tour de Sol was won by a team from Mercedes Benz with help from Alpha Real, a photovoltaic electronics company.

Thousands of onlookers crowded the roads to witness the world's first solar car race. Their enthusiastic cheers were a clear statement to Muntwyler: the timing was perfect.

All but four of the 58 entrants in the first Tour de Sol had completed the 368-kilometer race. Many others had expressed an interest in the competition. Everyone encouraged Muntwyler to organize another event to keep the concept alive. So, the Tour de Sol became an annual event in Europe, attracting more entrants, more spectators, and more media attention each year.

Impatient with leaders in the transportation industry, Tholstrup wanted to force technology forward. Determined to make a difference in the world's energy consumption, MacCready wanted to push technology to its outer limits. Eager to reach out to the people

Above: Driver Peter Bauer and his team leader Achim Kaden.

14

with solar technology, Muntwyler wanted to stimulate public awareness. Unwilling to accept any idea as "impossible," these three pioneers blazed a trail that would inspire thousands of other scientists and engineers to challenge the status quo. In striving for a brighter energy future, a cleaner environment, and new applications of advanced technologies, today's efforts to design and build solar cars have managed to surpass everyone's expectations.

Back in the United States, another young scientist was stirring up radical ideas. By 1990, the name James Worden had become almost synonymous with solar car racing in this country. Actually, he has been an inventor of sorts since the age of nine. Experimenting with solar cars was a logical extension of his natural inclination to build things with an unusual twist.

In conversation with 26-year-old James Worden, his seemingly laid-back manner soon gives way to an intense excitement about what he is doing. He is a dreamer, but he is also a tried and true realist. With patience and persistence, Worden tests and retests his ideas, constantly attempting to improve upon his own inventions.

As he tells it, the seeds for his current endeavors began in his elementary school years. He gives a lot of credit to his parents and a special third grade teacher whose influence was far-reaching. Worden is modest about his own achievements and gives credit to those around him quite generously. He is sure, though, that all the biographies he read as a youngster stimulated his motivation to succeed.

Worden first noticed solar cells in a Radio Shack store in his native Massachusetts in 1978. "They were the little two-square-centimeter size," he says, "And I bought all they had: four cells at $9.99 each." For some youngsters, this might have been an insignificant purchase. But for Worden, it led to the creation of solar-powered Lego toys, which he put together on his own just for the fun of it.

By the time he was ten years old, Worden had hooked up his electric train set to the solar cells. When the first rays of morning sunshine hit the cells mounted on the window, his trains would start zooming around the track. He had even figured out how to wire the batteries so he could store some of this plentiful solar energy. Worden's inventive mind and mechanical aptitude were already being put to good use. He was not about to miss any opportunities for innovation!

His next fascination was go-carts. Worden's parents were less than pleased when he created a total mess in the family garage. But their 12-year-old son had a clear mission, and it would have been impossible to dampen his enthusiasm. Mr. Worden, a patient man and truly proud father, claims that James was born an engineer, building with whatever materials were handy. Without the steady understanding and support of his parents, however, this young man might have had his wings clipped before soaring beyond the ordinary.

After devoting months of hard work to a gasoline-powered engine for his go-cart, including several burns and major mechanical problems, Worden stumbled upon some information about electric motors. Here was the solution for his machine on wheels. Satisfied beyond belief, his electrically-powered go-cart crafted of wood and cardboard was soon a reality. As he rode around in his new invention, he discovered the joy of racing.

Before long Worden realized a new desire. He wanted to build a solar electric car to drive on the streets. He is forever thankful for the yellow pages, because it was only after a thorough search there that Worden found a shop receptive to his request for a "motor hunt." Then came the tough part. He had to buy some solar cells, but he didn't have enough money. His parents were very skeptical of the idea. Finally, his mother came to the rescue. She bought him a big, 36-cell solar panel for $150, which he claims was "major money." This was the true beginning of Solectria I, the first in a whole line of solar-powered vehicles designed and built by James Worden.

In 1983, Worden entered Solectria I in a high school science fair. Capable of 20 mph (32 kph) speeds, his car could travel 25 miles (40 kms) on the solar energy collected in one day. After winning first prize at the State Science Quest, Worden said, "Wow! This is it!" He was convinced that he could do even better next time and immediately began work on Solectria II.

By then, Hans Tholstrup had finished his Solar Trek across Australia. The November 1983 issue of National Geographic magazine featured an article about his incredible journey. Worden read every word. Fascinated by Tholstrup's feat, he was determined to apply the lessons of the Quiet Achiever to his Solectria II. The aspiring engineer with the inventive spirit charged full speed ahead into solar car technology. When Worden was accepted into the Massachusetts Institute of Technology in 1985, he knew it was his science fair win with Solectria that secured him a place in his first-choice school.

James Worden in his Solectria IV solar racing car waiting for the starter to give him the signal to start the 1989 Tour de Sol.

The beautiful Swiss Alps provide a scenic background for the Tour de Sol.

1989 Tour de Sol

The objective of the Tour de Sol is to promote solar energy and solar electric vehicles for every-day use. To demonstrate the viability of the electric vehicles to the public, the route is chosen to climb through the mountains on purpose.

The five-day race, held every June, winds its way through the beautiful countryside stopping in towns and villages to display the cars to the public.

Panasonic's solar car shown in the winner's circle of the 1989 Tour de Sol.

1991 Tour de Sol

By 1991, the Swiss Tour de Sol was predominantly an electric vehicle race rather than a solar car race. The 1991 event had over 80 electric commuter vehicles of different types and only 6 solar powered race cars. Shown on this page are some of the urban, or "city" cars. These electric vehicles can drive over 50 miles on a single charge and make an ideal mode of transportation for commuting around town.

What moved Worden, the undergraduate engineering student, onto center stage with solar car racing? In April 1986, a friend at M.I.T. heard about a competitive event in Switzerland called the Tour de Sol. It didn't take much persuasion to talk him into entering this solar car race. Worden was delighted to have an opportunity to participate in a new kind of road rally.

Two months later, Worden was driving Solectria III in the Swiss Alps. At age 19, he had

For the first three days of the 1989 Swiss Tour de Sol, James Worden was leading. Above: Worden receives honors for winning day three.

built his first solar race car from the ground up, a car fit to compete with teams of professionals. While at the Tour de Sol, he got to know a whole new cadre of engineers who believed that solar electric vehicles were a healthy alternative to the internal combustion engine. The synergistic effect was extraordinary. For young Worden, this ten-day experience was the real-life equivalent of four graduate courses in applied technology.

Upon returning home to the States, Worden formed his own company to design and build solar cars. Named after his racing vehicles, Solectria's major objective was to produce solar electric commuter cars for everyday use. Solar racing continued to be a pathway to strive for excellence, but Worden's long-term goal was to change the driving habits of the buying public.

Far from M.I.T., students at a small college in southwestern Missouri were involved in a concurrent project that echoed Worden's ingenuity and determination. In Neosho, they too had read the article about the Quiet

Achiever in National Geographic. Chris Kalmbach, a graduate of Crowder College, was inspired by Hans Tholstrup's accomplishment crossing Australia. He suggested a challenge. Why not have a solar-powered car race across the United States?

Late in 1983, an air mail letter was sent from Missouri to Australia. Inside, there was an invitation for Tholstrup. If he could get to the United States, a Crowder car would race the Quiet Achiever from coast to coast.

As fate would have it, the Quiet Achiever did not make the trip. Determined to proceed full-steam ahead with their plans, a group of solar enthusiasts at Crowder mapped out the first TransAmerican Solar Auto Run (TSAR). When asked why, their response was, "Because it had not been done before."

Art Boyt, a faculty member at Crowder's engineering department, became the driving force behind this project. Equipped with a smile a mile wide, Boyt exudes a sense of genuine pleasure at being alive. An astute listener blessed with an abundance of sincerity, his calm demeanor melts away into wholehearted excitement whenever engaged in conversation about his unique projects.

A longtime believer in the untapped potential of alternative energy sources, Boyt was not only teaching about solar energy, but also experiencing its benefits. In the late seventies when solar had reached its hiatus, Boyt designed and built his own passive solar home. Actually, the final phase of construction resembled an old-fashioned barn-raising, with plenty of help on hand from Boyt's students, friends, and neighbors. His approach is indicative of the classic Missouri ethic that, "You can't do it unless you do it yourself."

When the house was finally finished, Boyt had a new home. But more significantly, he

James Worden (below, center) with his Solectria solar racing car just prior to the 1989 Swiss Tour de Sol. Standing to the left is team member Gil Pratt.

had also acquired a new friend who was to become a key element in his professional life.

Dan Eberle, an elementary school teacher who had some experience building houses, was hooked on solar after taking one of Boyt's classes at Crowder. Later, he participated in the construction of Boyt's solar home. Eberle's keen interest provided a natural link to Boyt's own zealous pursuit of applied solar technologies. They developed a mutual friendship, teaming their creative efforts for special projects.

Together, they make quite a pair. The antithesis of Boyt's modest stature, Eberle bears a close resemblance to a professional football player. With a wonderfully warm handshake and a rich baritone voice, his gregarious personality and human relations skills are an ideal complement to Boyt's technical background. Their relationship spans two decades. The synergy of their combined talent has yielded remarkable results in the world of solar car racing.

After consulting with Boyt, Kalmbach was sure the effort to build a solar car in the U.S. was well worth making. Along with Boyt and Eberle, he enlisted the support of Steve Tipton, Greg Brockman, and Doug Smith, students at Crowder College. Although Tipton did not know it then, this project was the starting point of an exciting seven-year commitment to solar racing.

Fueled by sheer enthusiasm, the Crowder solar car team spent three months designing the TSAR vehicle. They agreed upon three essential criteria: simplicity, reliability, and efficiency. Once they reached a consensus for the design, they found themselves immersed in a four-month-long construction project. Kalmbach donated $5,000 for expenses, and the team donated over 600 hours of precious time.

The fruit of their labor was a vehicle which measured 22 feet in length, 6 feet in width, and 28 inches in height. Sixteen Solarex modules comprised the solar array for the car, producing 640 watts of peak power in full sunlight. The 256-pound (116-kg) panel was positioned horizontally behind the low-slung driver's seat. In reality, this three-wheeler with the open cockpit could easily have been mistaken for an oversized tricycle hauling a fancy load of high-tech material.

Taking off from San Diego, California, the Crowder car left the Pacific coast in mid-July 1984. Averaging 20 mph (32 kph), it was accompanied by a van filled with spare parts, tools, and dedicated team members.

During each day of the Tour de Sol, the racers stop at mid-day to recharge their batteries from the sun. James Worden is shown here (below) taking a minute to have some lunch while his car soaks up some rays.

A gale force windstorm and severe flooding in Tacna, Arizona threatened to draw an early conclusion to this adventure. True to form, team members handled repairs and agreed to continue their journey. Renaming the car the Solar Phoenix, the five-member crew maintained their determination to make it all the way to the east coast. Forty-five days and 2,300 miles (3,700 kms) later, the Crowder team cruised into Jacksonville, Florida. To commemorate the occasion, they poured a bottle of Pacific Ocean water into the rolling surf of the Atlantic Ocean.

Boyt, Eberle, Tipton, and Kalmbach were ecstatic. Much to everyone's surprise, they had made it from coast to coast. Ironically, the epic

From left to right: Gina and Dan Eberle, Steve Tipton, and Art Boyt.

transcontinental crossing of the Phoenix served as a catalyst for future solar car escapades at Crowder College.

When they got wind of Tholstrup's announcement for the first World Solar Challenge, Crowder did not hesitate to reply. Their response was a new project, dubbed the Solar Trans-Australian Racer (STAR I).

This time, the team capitalized on prior experience with the Solar Phoenix. Under the capable leadership of Boyt and Eberle, a team of Crowder College students designed and constructed a new lightweight vehicle which traveled at 35 mph (56 kph) under cloudy skies and 50 mph (80 kph) in sunlight.

To get to Australia, the team utilized every possible means of fundraising, including traditional bake sales and t-shirt specials. Surely, their invincible optimism guaranteed their success. By November 1987, the Crowder team had a solar car as well as airplane tickets to Australia.

In the Outback of Australia, they had their first opportunity to challenge James Worden and Paul MacCready to the tune of Tholstrup's cheers. M.I.T. had entered the competition, and MacCready had teamed up with General Motors and Hughes Aircraft to race across the continent Down Under. It was an incredible competition.

In 1984, the "Solar Phoenix" (left) was the first solar car to be driven across the United States from San Diego, California to Jacksonville, Florida.

While driving in Arizona, a severe thunderstorm blew the "Solar Phoenix" off the road (above). Undaunted, the team pulled the car out of the water, repaired it, and continued on. Forty-five days and 2,300 miles later, the Crowder College team had reached the beach in Jacksonville, Florida (below).

III. Sunraycer Sets the Record

The sun-drenched continent of Australia was the site of the 1987 World Solar Challenge. Twenty-five teams from eight different countries were represented in this solar car competition. As planned by Tholstrup, the racers traveled from Darwin (in the north) to Adelaide (in the south), covering a distance of 1,867 miles (3,004 km). For the participants, it was an adventure they would never forget. Crossing the vast Australian Outback on solar power was the goal. Surviving the harsh conditions en route to the finish line was the reality.

The race included college students like those from M.I.T. and Crowder, as well as corporate giants like Ford Motor Company and Japan's Hoxan Corporation. General Motors was also one of the participants in the World Solar Challenge. Their decision to enter the competition is an interesting story. Later, their astounding first-place victory signaled the beginning of a dramatic turn for transportation technology in the United States.

GM's car, the "Sunraycer," surprised the world with its flawless cruise across the Australian Outback. Completing the race with a commanding 600-mile lead (965 km) in front of the second-place car, the Sunraycer made automotive history.

Building the Sunraycer was an ambitious project. Unlike any previous undertaking, the Sunraycer team had to develop plans for a car focused on maximum efficiency and minimum demand. Charged with building a moveable electric machine fueled by fickle sunshine, the team relied upon creativity and innovation. A great deal of the credit for the success of this project goes to Paul MacCready. No stranger to new frontiers, MacCready was a logical choice to head up the Sunraycer development team. His belief in "exploring five sides of a question" when researching new concepts helped him balance innovation and practicality.

The sunsets are magnificent in the Australian Outback. This picture shows the GM Sunraycer solar car team securing their car for the night.

Each day during the World Solar Challenge the solar cars must stop for ten minutes at a press stop. Teams can change drivers and check the status of their cars. Shown here is the GM Sunraycer on the first day of the 1987 race.

The GM entry which competed in the 1987 World Solar Challenge was no ordinary vehicle. The main objective of the design team was simple: build a solar car that would win the race. The course taken to accomplish this objective within the short eight-month time period involved a carefully-orchestrated series of events.

Sunraycer's unbeatable features revolved around the concepts of lightweight aerodynamics, efficient power electronics, and reliability. Achieving maximum power output as well as low aerodynamic drag required some important trade-offs in the design. Rather than utilize solar panels distinctly separate from the car's body to track the sun's rays (as some competitors had done), engineers mounted the solar cells directly on Sunraycer's streamlined body. With a unified shape, the Sunraycer slipped through the air, leaving a minimum amount of disturbed air flow behind. This also reduced the car's height and weight and increased its stability in strong crosswinds, a critical factor on Australian highways where monstrous 90-ton road trains (triple-trailer trucks) are a common sight.

To capture sunlight, Sunraycer's 12 separate solar cell arrays were mounted on its eight-square-meter surface panel. Most of the panel area (80 percent) contained gallium arsenide solar cells, which were 18 percent efficient. The rest of the panel area was covered with silicon solar cells, which were 16.5 percent efficient. Connected to the battery with peak power trackers, these 9,500 solar cells delivered 1,550 watts of power under midday sun.

An 11-pound (5 kg) Magnequench electric motor powered the car's drive train. Operating at 92 percent efficiency, this brushless, alternating-current motor provided four horsepower continuously and up to ten horsepower for short periods of time. Driven with electric power generated by the photovoltaic cells, Sunraycer's shiftless transmission and single-wheel drive train were unique features.

Silver-zinc batteries with their high energy density were an essential part of the car's electrical system. Weighing in at 60 pounds (27 kg), the batteries had three kilowatt-hours of storage capacity. With built-in instruments to monitor the operating conditions of the electrical components, the Sunraycer team was able to make optimal use of the limited energy supply from the car's batteries.

Sunraycer's total weight equaled a mere 397 pounds (180 kg). The exterior of the car was constructed from a sandwich of Kevlar-Nomex-Kevlar, two rigid, lightweight materials known for strength. The area on which the solar cells were mounted was made with high-temperature epoxy to withstand the excessively high temperatures of sunlight. The chassis and frame consisted of aluminum tubing.

To say that Sunraycer's tires held up the car is an understatement of their importance. These thin, slick bicycle tires decreased rolling resistance by approximately one-third of standard automobile tires. The tires had a significant effect on overall efficiency, and they helped the Sunraycer roll on to victory in Australia.

Ironically, Sunraycer's stunning first-place finish in the 1987 World Solar Challenge was not its most important victory. Instead, this was Sunraycer's beginning as a living legend, a key element in a public awareness program which would ultimately reach millions. The tiny vehicle that resembled a shiny, oversized extraterrestrial beetle proceeded to become a magnificent showcase of advanced technology. The synergy of the GM-Hughes-AeroVironment endeavor had produced a real winner.

Upon its return to the States, Sunraycer made its debut on the grounds of the U.S. Capitol in Washington, D.C., where it was cheered by Congressmen as a significant achievement. From there, it went on to General Motors headquarters in Detroit and then to the California Museum of Science and Industry in Los Angeles. Apparently, the car was just getting warmed up for further excitement. The Sunraycer was to play a leading role as a showcase of innovative car design for the energy-conscious public.

Identified as the "pace car of the future," Sunraycer was chosen as the lead vehicle in the Tournament of Roses parade in Pasadena on January 1, 1988. Like a glimmering blue ladybug bedecked with yellow roses, it brought rousing cheers from more than one million viewers.

In the next 17 months, the Sunraycer appeared in more than 250 events, including auto shows, museum displays, and professional conferences. Newspapers all over the world carried the story of this solar powered supercar, and it was featured in 14 different publications and several documentary films.

To accomplish one of its stated objectives "to stimulate interest in scientific and technical education," General Motors developed an ambitious educational program that reached virtually every elementary and secondary school in the nation. Instructional materials packages comprised of a 26-page teacher's manual, student handouts, a documentary film, and computer software were distributed to educators all across the U.S. The software featured an interactive game in which players could try their skills "driving" a solar powered vehicle in simulated race conditions. As a result, thousands of school children experienced the excitement of the race and got a glimpse of the technology behind Sunraycer's success. Students were introduced to concepts related to energy issues, science, math, and geography. They were taught how these skills were applied in the solar car race.

Although impossible to document, thousands of young people may have been influenced by these educational materials. Mailings to elementary schools numbered over 80,000 and those to secondary schools over 37,000. The ideas which inspired the creation of the Sunraycer reached a whole new generation of future scientists and engineers.

At the university level, the Sunraycer team produced materials for an engineering course, distributing the information to colleges and universities all across the United States. In addition, they visited nearly 50 schools to share their experiences in building and racing a solar powered car and to describe the technology behind the Sunraycer's amazing performance in Australia.

Then, something very special happened. In the process of reaching out to university students, General Motors made a surprising decision to promote a new and innovative hands-

Driver Molly Brennan (right) shows some young students the trophy on Capitol Hill after winning the World Solar Challenge.

FIG. 1: 1990 GM SUNRAYCE ROUTE

FINISH

MASON, MI
July 18

WARREN, MI
(GM TECH CENTER)
July 19

INDIANAPOLIS, IN
July 16

GREENVILLE, OH
July 17

LOUISVILLE, KY
July 15

BOWLING GREEN, KY
July 14

SPRING HILL, TN
July 13

HALEYVILLE, AL
July 12

MONTGOMERY, AL
July 11

TALLAHASSEE, FL
July 10

FLORAL CITY, FL
July 9

LAKE BUENA VISTA, FL   START
July 9

Below: The University of Maryland's solar car during wind tunnel tests.

on educational program. On December 5, 1988, General Motors announced the GM SUN-RAYCE USA, a transcontinental solar car race for university students. With support from the U.S. Department of Energy (DOE), Chevrolet Motor Division, and the Society of Automotive Engineers (SAE), elaborate plans were made for this dramatic national event.

Universities and colleges across North America were invited to submit proposals to enter the Sunrayce. Over 2,100 schools were contacted. More than 100 indicated initial interest in participating. Assured by these numbers, GM was confident that sponsoring a "scientific sporting event" was a winning idea.Like many other American companies, GM wanted to entice more students to choose science, math, and engineering as career paths. Knowing that less than one percent of U.S. college graduates become engineers compared with Japan's four percent was significant motivation for GM's drive to move this project forward. Perhaps this opportunity to design, build, and race solar cars would become the equivalent of working in a mobile laboratory. Maybe, just maybe, this hands-on experience with tangible results would motivate greater numbers of students to push technology toward new frontiers. Ultimately, this would yield measurable advances in our capacity to meet today's transportation needs. It might also make a world of difference in our application of renewable energy options.

The formal Request for Proposals (RFPs) went out in December 1988. Teams were required to describe the following tasks related to the development of solar electric vehicles which would compete in GM SUNRAYCE USA:

- funding and fundraising efforts
- team organization
- formulation of vehicle design concepts
- acquisition of vehicle components
- building the vehicle "from the ground up"
- evaluation of vehicle performance
- conducting reliability and durability tests
- selection and training of drivers
- planning a racing strategy

TABLE 1: GM SUNRAYCE USA COMPETITORS

Arizona State University	Drexel University	University of Texas-Austin
California State Polytechnic University, Pomona	Florida Institute of Technology	University of Maryland
California State Polytechnic University, San Luis Obispo	Iowa State University	University of Michigan
California State University, Los Angeles	Mankato State University	University of North Texas
California State University, Northridge	Massachusetts Institute of Technology	University of Ottawa
Clarkson University	Rochester Institute of Technology	University of Pennsylvania
Colorado State University	Rose-Hulman Institute of Technology	University of Waterloo
Crowder College	Stanford University	Villanova University
Dartmouth College	Stark Technical College	Virginia Tech
		Western Michigan-Jordan College Energy Institute
		Western Washington University
		Worcester Polytechnic Institute

A total of 65 proposals were submitted, a healthy response to this request for a very unusual undertaking. Here were 65 teams of aspiring engineers who intended to learn to race and to race to learn. The proposal selection process involved representatives from GM, AeroVironment, DOE, Hughes, SAE, and Chevrolet. Their assignment was to review the proposals and rate them according to these criteria:

- organization and project planning
- technical depth, components, and materials
- vehicle testing and driver training
- logistics

The task turned out to be far from easy, as many of the proposals were well-done and demonstrated real potential for success. The difficult decision-making process involved figuring out which teams might really make it to the starting line.

In April 1989, GM announced the 32 teams chosen to compete in the SUNRAYCE. To recognize the initial efforts of these students, a special race workshop was held. The teams were honored at the workshop and presented with "seed money" to start work on their solar cars. Each team received $5,000 from GM and $2,000 from DOE, modest beginnings for ambitious projects. The recipients' broad smiles and bubbling enthusiasm were indicative of their genuine commitment to do their very best in this "race for the future."

Eagerly accepting their positions at the leading edge of innovative technology, the teams pursued their dreams of winning SUNRAYCE with gusto and perseverance. General Motors kept in touch with a monthly SUNRAYCE Newsletter, and teams were encouraged to contact race sponsors with questions as their projects moved forward.

What happened in the next 14 months is a dramatic documentary of collaborative energy.

For 32 teams of students, SUNRAYCE participation became a continuing saga of special coursework and hands-on experiences. At the same time, these young men and women were addressing a critical problem facing our modern, highly mobile society: how to meet the world's insatiable appetite for energy by shifting dependence away from nature's limited nonrenewable resources, like oil and coal, toward renewable natural resources, such as solar power. Closely linked to this goal was the desire to discover how we can conserve precious energy resources by following Sunraycer's stunning achievement of "doing more with less."

If imagination and ingenuity are the keys that unlock the door to the future, then SUNRAYCE provided a port of entry to some of America's best and brightest minds. The outstanding efforts of the 32 teams chosen to compete in this solar car race showed that this country still has what it takes to make technological leaps toward the 21st century. Who would have thought it possible to drive 1,644 miles on the power of a hair dryer? This is the stuff of which dreams are made.

Professor David Holloway shows his University of Maryland students how their solar car will be designed.

When the 32 university teams arrived in Orlando, Florida for the start of GM SUNRAYCE USA, many students had to continue work on their cars to get them in top running condition. Shown here are the California State at Northridge's "CSUN Blazer" (above), the University of North Texas's "Centennial" (right), and University of Pennsylvania's "Solsation," (below).

IV: Students Prepare to Race for the Future

After the honor and fanfare of the SUNRAYCE workshop, 32 student teams faced a challenging reality. The mood in April 1989 was incredibly upbeat. Now, 14 months of hard work loomed ahead. The teams would have liked access to a "how-to" book on solar race car technology, but no such reference existed. They were on their own, seeking out resources and drawing upon their own knowledge of applied science, mathematics, and engineering. As it turned out, moving from concepts on paper to wheels on the road was no simple task.

Teams had to consider design trade-offs and functionally compatible systems. They also had practical problems to overcome, such as how they would secure adequate funding for their ambitious projects. Suddenly, many of the students felt like they were enrolled in a crash course on survival in the real world.

Being on a SUNRAYCE team entailed much more than cramming for a tough exam or writing a research paper. Those who participated began to understand the true meaning of the words ingenuity, commitment, cooperation, collaboration, and persistence. Students who joined SUNRAYCE teams had different reasons for participation, but there was one compelling common denominator for all - learning. SUNRAYCE offered an exciting hands-on experience which had relevance for the nation's future.

A solar race car is somewhat like a hybrid, a combination of transportation technology and advanced solid state electronic technology. Similar to the electric automobiles of the early 20th century, a solar car is powered by electricity. Unlike its predecessors, a solar car uses only sunshine for fuel. Running on charged batteries, it requires no gasoline and emits no pollutants. As long as there is sunlight, a solar car constantly refuels. Photovoltaic cells on the car collect and convert the energy from sunlight directly into electricity. Nonreliance upon any form of nonrenewable fossil fuel makes the vehicle completely self-sufficient.

The propulsion system of a solar race car consists of three basic components: solar cells, batteries, and an electric motor. In designing their vehicles, teams had some critical choices to make regarding these components.

SOLAR CELLS

Solar cells are solid-state semiconductor devices made up primarily of silicon atoms. When rays of sunlight, or photons, strike an orbiting electron, enough energy is absorbed to free it from the nucleus. The freed electrons "escape" or migrate to the surface. Wires draw them off in the form of electricity. The phenomenon occurs instantaneously, whenever light of any kind strikes the cells.

The last decade has shown significant progress in solar cell development. In 1980, silicon solar cells were six percent efficient. Highly advanced aerospace cells were 12 percent efficient. Ten years later, efficiency had doubled. Silicon cells are 12-14 percent efficient, and aerospace cells approach 20 percent.

Solar cells are cut from purified silicon ingots (right). Individual solar cells are connected together to make modules (below) which can be deployed in large systems to provide clean electricity for homes and cities.

Solar cells are critical, providing the horsepower to propel the solar electric vehicles. The greater their efficiency, the more horsepower available and the higher the speed. For a typical solar car, an array producing 10 percent more electricity (from 1,000 watts to 1,100 watts, for example) will result in a vehicle which is 2-3 miles per hour faster. Over the 1,644-mile SUNRAYCE route, this saves the car approximately six hours in total driving time; a difference that could mean placing in the winner's circle.

BATTERIES

Batteries store electricity to power the solar car on cloudy days and to provide extra power for acceleration (when passing other vehicles or ascending hills). Batteries provide a buffer between the solar array and the electric motor. If a direct connection between the solar panels and the motor were used, the car would come to a halt every time its cells were shaded.

Actually, the motor draws electricity from the batteries while the solar cells charge the batteries. For top performance, racing teams calculate the average speed, based on available sunlight, that draws battery power equivalent to that being replenished by the photovoltaic cells. This process ensures that battery power is not totally depleted.

Solar racing strategy includes calculating the necessary energy for the entire route and then determining the optimum average speed to wear the battery power down to zero dur-ing the last few miles of the course. Finishing second or third with energy still available in the batteries results in no dividend.

MOTOR

In a solar car, an electric motor provides the mechanical torque to turn the drive wheel and propel the vehicle. Each SUNRAYCE team sought a lightweight, highly efficient motor for its car. The standard solar car array produces electricity equivalent to one horsepower. Typically, the batteries could produce up to 10 horsepower at full acceleration. The optimum design, therefore, calls for a motor to run efficiently at one to two horsepower, delivering up to 10-15 horsepower when needed for short periods of time.

Compared with the internal combustion engine (ICE) on an equal basis, an electric motor can provide more torque. Furthermore, its 80-95 percent efficiency by far surpasses the 20-30 percent efficiency of the ICE. This helps explain how solar cars can travel literally thousands of miles on the power of a standard portable hair dryer.

The main objective for each team was to build a car that would win the SUNRAYCE. Winning the race meant having a high-performance vehicle which made optimal use of available solar energy. Design considerations included hundreds of trade-offs, but certain elements were essential in the ultimate achievement of racing the total distance in the shortest amount of time.

Reliability was an important design factor

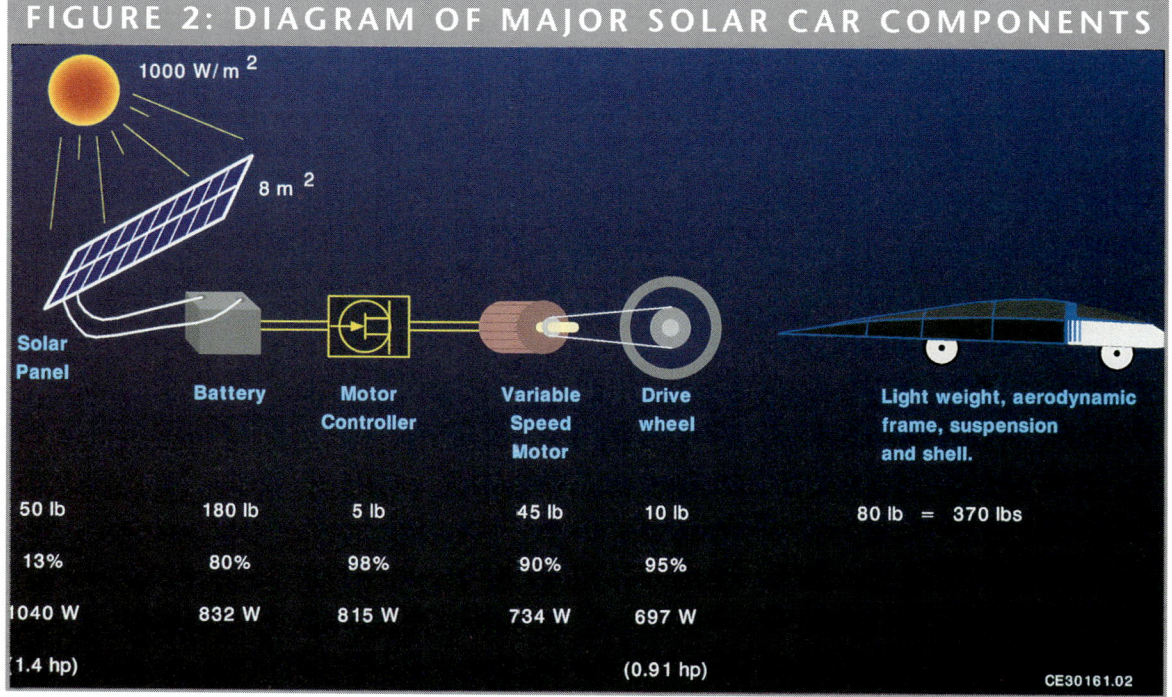

FIGURE 2: DIAGRAM OF MAJOR SOLAR CAR COMPONENTS

	Solar Panel	Battery	Motor Controller	Variable Speed Motor	Drive wheel	Light weight, aerodynamic frame, suspension and shell.
Weight	50 lb	180 lb	5 lb	45 lb	10 lb	80 lb = 370 lbs
Efficiency	13%	80%	98%	90%	95%	
Power	1040 W	832 W	815 W	734 W	697 W	
	(1.4 hp)				(0.91 hp)	

CE30161.02

for all teams. A vehicle which performed well without any major breakdowns would cover the race distance in less time. Some teams recognized the importance of reliability before the race began; advance preparation yielded measurable results. Teams that did not evaluate vehicle performance sufficiently paid a high cost in time during SUNRAYCE.

The overall shape of a solar car is another important design factor. Teams had to determine how and where they would mount the solar cells for maximum energy gain. They also had to decide how to maintain low weight and minimal aerodynamic drag while accommodating solar panels. Basic shape options included: 1) vehicles with solar panels separate from the car body; 2) unified aerodynamic vehicles with solar cells mounted directly on the car body (similar to Sunraycer design); and 3) catamaran

University of Maryland solar car team member Henry Ya gives the car an early test drive before the body is finished.

FIGURE 3: CATEGORIES OF SOLAR CAR DESIGN

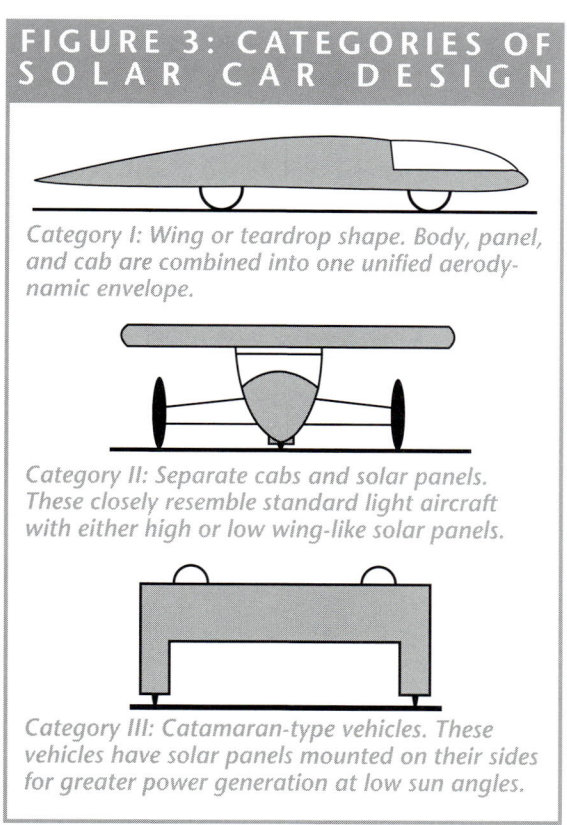

Category I: Wing or teardrop shape. Body, panel, and cab are combined into one unified aerodynamic envelope.

Category II: Separate cabs and solar panels. These closely resemble standard light aircraft with either high or low wing-like solar panels.

Category III: Catamaran-type vehicles. These vehicles have solar panels mounted on their sides for greater power generation at low sun angles.

type vehicles with solar panels mounted on sides and on top of the car body.

A solar car generally operates on only 700-1,500 watts of power, or about one to two horsepower. This means that low aerodynamic drag is extremely important. Some SUNRAYCE teams did extensive wind tunnel testing to determine modifications necessary to achieve the lowest possible drag coefficient for their vehicles. Even the slightest change in the shape of a solar car can result in significant differences in performance during a race. With efficiency the primary influence for

a winning performance, low aerodynamic drag was a critical element.

Keeping a solar car's weight down is essential as well. Lower weight requires less energy, helping a car accelerate faster and climb hills at higher speeds. Teams investigated various lightweight materials and composite construction techniques to minimize the weight of their vehicles. Some sought the support of chemical companies and aerospace industries to research the best available materials for fabrication of their cars.

Another design trade-off for solar cars is the choice of tires. Besides transporting the car body, tires have a tremendous impact on overall vehicle efficiency. Radial automobile tires driving on rough pavement result in 0.90-1.1 percent drag for the load carried. But, for bicycle tires, only 0.55-0.65 percent of the load results in drag. The thin tread increases the rolling resistance and yields much lower weight and aerodynamic drag than conventional tires. Most teams used bicycle tires on their cars. They discovered that not all tires are created equal.

Teams had a vast array of design criteria to evaluate. Once they began building their cars, continuous evaluation and modification were necessary. Like never-ending obstacle courses, SUNRAYCE projects required ongoing observation and strategy-adjustment to meet unpredictable challenges.

While students were absorbed in designing and building their cars, the "human factor" became a vital aspect. Leadership was a must for every team, providing a pivotal force which kept the projects focused and on schedule. Cooperation and collaboration among team members was also crucial. Those that learned to work together during the development stages reaped huge benefits later when balancing the stresses and demands of the rigorous 11-day race.

For James Worden, designing and building a solar car for the SUNRAYCE was second nature. When GM's announcement came out in December 1989, he was already immersed in solar-powered transportation. A mechanical engineering student at M.I.T., he had been tinkering with solar electric vehicles since his teenage years. His workshop, tucked into an old building on campus grounds, was a makeshift laboratory frequented by fellow engineering students. A visit to his "headquarters" makes Worden's desire to be the Henry Ford of solar automobiles actually seem more realistic than outlandish.

By 1989, Worden had already built a half-dozen solar electric vehicles, including Solectria I through IV. Two of his cars, Solectria III and IV, had been pitted against international competition in the Swiss Tour de Sol. Another Worden vehicle, a small solar commuter car which he used for everyday driving, was a common sight in Cambridge, Massachusetts. At age 22, this young engineer was probably one of the foremost experts in solar car technology in the United States. Worden had a huge supply of ingenuity and plenty of hands-on experience with vehicle construction. Blessed with an unbelievable ability to troubleshoot mechanical problems, any breakdowns would be attacked and repaired in a remarkably short time.

The M.I.T. team had planned to build a car named the "Galaxy" even before they wrote their SUNRAYCE proposal. Worden wanted to design a vehicle to set a new speed record for solar cars. The Sunraycer holds that record at 75 mph (120 kph). Similar to the precursor Solectria models, the car has a slender unified aerodynamic body with solar cells mounted on top. The Galaxy driver's seat is noticeable only by the clear plastic bubble which pops up out of the sleek upper surface of the vehicle. The entire vehicle weighs a mere 350 pounds (159 kg). Worden built it primarily for speed rather than long-distance durability.

By May 1990, the Galaxy was still not finished. Detailed plans were on the drawing board, and most of the parts were partially assembled and tested. But the Galaxy was not yet on the road. True to form, Worden and his team pulled it all together in a mere six weeks. When it was time for the SUNRAYCE qualifying laps at the Daytona Speedway, the Galaxy was not on the scene. Not until the next day did the Galaxy make its appearance, qualifying for the SUNRAYCE only 12 hours before the official start.

With just one day left before the start of GM SUNRAYCE USA, the MIT solar car team finally had their car ready. Shown above is the "Galaxy" being rolled out by team members for final inspections.

Crowder College's "Star II" on display at the EPCOT Center in Orlando, Florida.

CROWDER COLLEGE

With two generations of solar-powered vehicles under their wing, SUNRAYCE participation seemed a logical extension for students at Crowder College. Sparked by the optimism and determination of faculty members Art Boyt and Dan Eberle, these students personified motivation and dedication. They wanted to go beyond learning ABOUT history and technology. They wanted to MAKE history with state-of-the-art technology.

The successful cross-continental trip of the Phoenix in 1984 had put the small Ozark town of Neosho, Missouri on the map of solar pioneers. That bright beginning, however, turned out to be only the first chapter of an exciting and dramatic story. Three years later, a team of students was prepared to harness the bright sun of the Australian Outback.

In 1987, Crowder's entry in the first World Solar Challenge, the Star I, had a surprising 8th place finish in a field of 24. Exhilarated by their achievement in Australia, the Crowder team looked forward to a continuation of their historic solar adventures by entering SUNRAYCE.

Not accustomed to resting on their laurels, Boyt and Eberle charged ahead with new enthusiasm. Dissatisfied with the gloomy predicament of our energy future with fossil fuels, they wanted to provide their students with practical experiences managing real-world problems. Solar racing was an open door to the future, and, with their students, they had the key. As plans for the prototype of the Star II proceeded, both the students and faculty members were proud to have devised a model which represented a striking contrast with the Sunrayer design. In fact, the Star II was based on an entirely different aerodynamic concept that Boyt had read about in a 1948 Popular Science article on aircraft design.

The Crowder car is not the typical solar vehicle with the sleek space-age image. Approached head-on, the car resembles an oversized, upside-down shoebox missing its front panel. A closer look reveals two clear bubbles poised on opposing sides of the top of the car and skirted wheels underneath. The Star II shape is labeled an "inverted U" with a slick, open underbelly. A two-person car, the Star II allows for steady air flow beneath its catamaran-type body, reducing turbulence and aerodynamic drag. Solar cells from Siemens and Applied Solar Energy cover the sides and top of the car, providing the 1,200 watts of peak power needed to maintain its average cruising speed of 40 miles per hour (64 kph).

The Crowder team that arrived in Orlando, Florida for the SUNRAYCE start included well-seasoned experts on solar cars. Student team member Steve Tipton, for example, had a long history of involvement with Crowder's efforts to cross the U.S. and Australia on sunpower. A modest, soft-spoken young man, Tipton had developed a rare understanding of what solar racing strategy entailed. His pivotal leadership helped build a highly-committed team well-versed in coaxing the most out of the sun's unpredictable bounty of energy.

To roll on to victory, Tipton worked hard to show the student drivers how to bring out the best from the STAR II. Furthermore, their vehicle had been carefully tested in the laboratory and on the road. When they pulled up to the green flag at the EPCOT starting line, Crowder team members were comfortably familiar with Star II's mechanical components and operation in motion.

If anyone were to describe this group, they might refer to them as "together," both professionally and personally. In fact, Eberle claims that the group is more like a close-knit family than a racing team. Students maintained steady support for the project, despite the demands of long hours and sheer hard work.

Going beyond the boundaries of what was required, engineering student Tipton summed up the experience quite aptly. He says that SUNRAYCE was "the opportunity of a lifetime which would lead to a lifetime of opportunity."

UNIVERSITY OF MARYLAND

The College Park campus of the University of Maryland sits astride the nation's capitol, flanking the beltway which encircles Washington, D.C. For the Maryland team, GM's announcement of the solar car competition represented an awesome task worth pursuing.

David Holloway, professor of mechanical engineering, saw SUNRAYCE as an opportunity for University of Maryland students to compete with other prestigious schools of engineering. Students would gain valuable experience designing and building a sunshine spe-

University of Maryland team members prepare to test their solar array. The tarp was used to shade the array prior to testing it so it remained as cool as possible.

cial with a simultaneous boost to their self-esteem. Confident and full of spirit, Maryland's aspiring engineers accepted the challenge with serious dedication.

To quote team member and driver Bill Raynor, "The SUNRAYCE project was the big time." He describes his participation as "a chance to be involved with the search for solutions to one of the world's most pressing problems - the energy crisis; to do something that really made a difference."

The thoughts of the other 25 team members echoed his sentiments. Students eagerly embraced the opportunity to take theories learned in the classroom and put them to practical use; to put their brainpower to a real-world test on the open road.

Close proximity to Washington meant that the University of Maryland team could be on hand when the GM Sunraycer was formally presented to the Smithsonian Institution in the fall of 1989. Shaking hands with GM President Robert Stempel and Gossamer inventor Paul MacCready, team members beamed with pride in their matching bright red sweaters. As they positioned themselves next to that marvel on wheels, the glistening sunpowered ladybug which had shattered the world's image of transportation alternatives, the Maryland team was sure they too would set some records in the next 12 months. The first prototype of their car, the "Pride of Maryland," had already been tested in the University of Maryland wind tunnel. Somehow, they knew they had a winner.

Holloway and his students chose the Sunraycer design as the standard to beat. Team member Rob Piacesi says, "Nothing sticks like sticking with a winner." An exhaustive search of existing solar car designs and a steady-state simulation code helped the team finalize their decision.

The Pride of Maryland is a super-streamlined vehicle with a rounded frontal area, flat rear panel, and gently sloping tail. The team's commitment to a "no compromises" approach meant using space-grade silicon cells. Solarex Corporation agreed to sponsorship, providing 2,300 photovoltaic cells for the car. The entire vehicle weighs only 415 pounds, making it one of the lightest cars in the SUNRAYCE.

The finishing touches of the Pride of Maryland were not complete until just before qualifying at the Daytona Speedway, two days prior to the start of the race. The Maryland car proved to be a masterful combination of engineering. The Pride, clocked at 52 miles per hour at the Daytona, qualified for the pole position. Team members' spirits soared. They were off and running.

CLARKSON UNIVERSITY

At Clarkson University, tucked away in rural Potsdam, New York, the solar car odyssey began in the fall of 1988. Kindled by a desire for cleaner transportation alternatives, a group of students invited James Worden to come to Clarkson. Led by Professor Eric Thacher, they organized a seminar on solar electric vehicles. Worden, with his established reputation as a solar car designer and racer, was the speaker.

In December of that year, two months after Worden's energizing presentation, the SUNRAYCE announcement arrived in the mail. Clarkson University was well prepared. A team of students and faculty members formed to write a proposal, working diligently for the next six weeks. When news of their acceptance into the race reached them, they were elated.

Then, all of a sudden, the idea of designing and constructing a solar car from the ground up loomed like an over ambitious monster. Students faced conflicting commitments: final exams, summer jobs, vacation plans, and now, unflinching dedication to the SUNRAYCE project. Faculty advisors encouraged students to view it as a "mature decision," an opportunity to participate in a genuine problem-solving activity with real-world value. Six students stayed in Potsdam all summer. Four faculty members joined them for weekly meetings. Together, they discussed design trade-offs and fund-raising possibilities. By September 1989, they were well on their way with SUNRAYCE preparations.

Clarkson's car is named "Kalahkwaneha," a name borrowed from the Mohawk Indian language. It means "belonging to the sun." They said they chose it because Native Americans have shown great respect for nature. The Clarkson team conducted wind tunnel testing over a lengthy period before making a final decision about the shape of the car. Finally, they settled on having a separate solar array mounted on top of a streamlined car body. Then, just one month before the SUNRAYCE, they changed the body design, undertaking four-weeks' worth of furious activity.

This time period included a transformation in the transmission as well. The team decided on a direct drive system on the left

rear wheel. But they were disappointed with the "slippery" performance of aluminum drive gears. Their unique solution was a hockey puck attached to the shaft of the motor, forced against the wheel with a spring. They were worried about slippage in wet weather, but lacked the time for sufficient testing. So, off to Florida they went, geared up for a game of "sunshine hockey."

The University of Clarkson named their solar car (above) "Kalahkwaneha," which means in Mohawk Indian language: "belonging to the sun." They said they chose it because Native Americans have shown great respect for nature.

WESTERN WASHINGTON UNIVERSITY

For some people, the compelling desire to build movable objects on wheels seems practically innate. Michael Seal has devoted a good part of his life to vehicle design and fabrication, almost as if this were an instinctual fascination. Although his name conjures up images of biological creatures, automotive technology is the name of the game for Seal. At Western Washington University, which straddles the U.S.-Canadian border between Vancouver and Seattle, Seal is an engineering professor. He is also the founder and director of the Vehicle Research Institute (VRI), an arm of Western Washington's Engineering Technology Program.

Since 1974, Seal has worked with engineering students to plan and construct Viking automobiles and specially-commissioned prototype vehicles. The decision to have a Western Washington entry in the SUNRAYCE was part of a larger strategy to give WWU's Vehicle Research Institute a boost in becoming a major center of automotive research.

The Western Washington team of 32 named their car the Viking XX. Of all the cars in the SUNRAYCE, its design is undoubtedly the most radical. Looking more like a large tilted cereal box atop a giant bean pod than an automobile, the Viking XX is a real eye-catcher.

One wonders how on earth they ever came up with this design. Apparently, Seal introduced the concept of a solar car to his students and asked them to share their ideas

for vehicle design, no matter how wild they might be. After sifting through all the suggestions for a winning vehicle, they were left with only two possibilities: a car very similar to the Sunraycer or a modified catamaran with an angled solar panel. According to Seal, replicating an existing car did not represent sufficient potential for learning anything new about solar car design and technology. He preferred taking a totally different approach. And that's how the awesome-looking Viking XX came into being.

To generate maximum power, the Western Washington car has a larger solar array than most, allowable because it is a two-person vehicle. To capture maximum sunlight on its sloping panel (fixed at 30 degrees from the horizontal), the car can be driven in either direction. For morning cruising on the south-to-north SUNRAYCE route, the Viking drives with its panel tilted eastward. In the afternoon, the Viking was turned around for westward exposure of its array.

The pod which houses the two back-to-back drivers seems custom-made for five-year-old children, but somehow two university-age students managed to squeeze inside. Weighing 750 pounds, the Western Washington car was one of the heaviest entries in the SUNRAYCE. But, it was also one of the most powerful.

At the Viking's unveiling in April 1990, Washington Governor Booth Gardner called the car "the wave of the future," referring to the car as a "source of tremendous pride" for the university and for the community. Under Seal's tutelage, the Viking team acquired knowledge and skills far beyond their own expectations.

CAL POLY POMONA

California State Polytechnic University at Pomona, commonly referred to as Cal Poly Pomona, was Michael Shelton's alma mater. A

The most clever solar car was designed and built by the team from Western Washington University. It was a two-person car that drove in both directions. The two drivers sat back-to-back in the side pod. (top photo) The large solar array was fixed at a 30° angle. During the morning, the car drove with the array pointing towards the eastern sky to collect maximum sunlight. At noon (middle), the team members would lift the car and turn it around so it would drive in the opposite direction, with the array facing the western sky. Named the "Viking XX," it had the largest solar array ever built on a solar car (right).

Cal Poly Pomona's "Solar Flair" was an early favorite to win the GM SUNRAYCE USA but ran into trouble the very first day, finishing in 22nd place (for that day) out of 32 teams.

1967 graduate of aerospace engineering, he then went on to become a professor of mechanical engineering at Cal Poly Pomona. Two decades later, he asked his vehicle design class if they were interested in writing a proposal for a solar car competition. Engineering student Jon Harvey recalls, "I raised my hand, and my whole life changed." Harvey eventually became the team leader, studying for his master's degree while building the Cal Poly solar car.

What began as a group of five or six eager beavers turned into a diversified group of 150 students and 30 faculty advisors. They were committed to one goal: outperform all the other cars in the SUNRAYCE. CaPSET (Cal Poly Pomona's Solar Energy Team) took on the task of designing and building the solar car under Shelton's leadership.

In the earliest stages, enthusiastic team members wired a solar panel plated with silicon cells to a golf cart. Then, they drove it around the Cal Poly Pomona campus, tilting the panel to determine the energy gain at various angles. For many students, that was just the beginning of action-packed days accompanied by sleepless nights.

Harvey says the students are motivated by the "cutting edge atmosphere." He contends that "being in on the ground floor is a distinct advantage."

The monthly CaPSET newsletter kept the team informed and highlighted major accomplishments of the project. Shelton estimates that team members logged in nearly 75,000 person-hours working on the solar car. His smile reveals his true feelings when he says, "It's exciting to see what a bunch of students can do when they have the desire."

The team's subgroups included fundraising, public relations, communications, fabrication, computer simulation, solar, mechanical design, power management, and signal processing. There was even a student with the title "Human Factors." Jonathan Kim's job was to integrate the human into the vehicle, based on ergonomic principles. Kim believes the SUNRAYCE project was a winning approach to learning, since "competitiveness is more tangible than research and development."

After five months of deliberation, CaPSET settled on the car design, with construction beginning in September 1989. The "Solar Flair" is a unified aerodynamic envelope with a long sloping convex tail covered with 2,300 solar cells.

Bob Solorzano created a computer simulation of the SUNRAYCE route to calculate how fast the car could go each day without depleting the batteries. His model used aerodynamic data, topographic data, and weather reports....all part of the team's hi-tech effort for the Solar Flair.

Cal Poly Pomona raised approximately half a million dollars in cash and donated materials. Perhaps it was the sight of the smog-laden San Gabriel Valley that pushed this team to excel. That constant reminder of the environmental damage inflicted by the internal combustion engine motivated this group to support the idea of a cleaner transportation alternative.

UNIVERSITY OF MICHIGAN

In the spring of 1989, the sprawling Ann Arbor campus of the University of Michigan witnessed the metamorphosis of a small group of action-oriented students into a large diversified team of solar car racers. Bill Kaliardos spearheaded the SUNRAYCE proposal-writing effort, but it was Susan Fancy who mobilized the team to get a jump start on the project. Within two weeks of the GM workshop, she had rallied her organizational skills, laying the groundwork for a year of unprecedented challenges.

Fancy recalls being an auto enthusiast way back in her childhood. By the time she entered high school, she had restored several old cars in the family garage. At age 16, she acquired her first sports car, a 1968 Chevy Camaro. Completely overtaken by this early love affair, she rebuilt the vehicle for her own road use.

A longtime member of the Sports Car Club of America and the Society of Automotive Engineers, Fancy's dedication to automobiles supercedes any whimsical interest or "passing fancy." Following a period in which she "lavished her attention on muscle cars," Fancy had her first experience with a professional race, one with an environmental slant. She was selected as the project manager of a student group to develop a University of Michigan car for the 1989 GM Methanol Marathon. Fancy was charged with coordinating the team's efforts to convert a production vehicle to operate efficiently on methanol fuel in a 1,000-mile competition.

Fancy claims the project was only "marginally successful." And she wanted another chance to apply what she had learned; a chance to prove she could "do it right." The SUNRAYCE was just the opportunity she needed.

Fancy realized that the solar car project would be radically different than any of her previous automotive experiences. Immediately, she enlisted the support of fellow mechanical engineering students for car design and manufacturing. Then, she recruited help from five University of Michigan schools in the largest-ever student project at Ann Arbor. The team of 110 included students of journalism, law, business, and art, in addition to the core team of industrial, electrical, and mechanical engineers. The mix of talent was impressive.

The Michigan team understood the importance of financial support. Fancy would repeatedly say, "Money counts. It buys better cells, better batteries, and more efficient components." Fancy's tight organization, unwavering attention to detail, and ability to maintain professional attitudes among team members convinced would-be sponsors that this group could deliver. And deliver they did. Successful marketing and public relations activities enabled the team to raise over $600,000 in donations and in-kind support.

The University of Michigan team studied the Sunraycer design, but their vehicle, the "Sunrunner," is no clone. The team decided on an unusual low-drag shape, a modified

ABOVE: *The University of Michigan's "Sunrunner." The Michigan team was one of the most well prepared teams to arrive in Orlando for inspections, spending hours testing their solar car on the road. Weeks before the race they could be seen driving in and around their home town of Ann Arbor.*

RIGHT: *Susan Fancy (kneeling front center) with her team during the "Sunrunner's" unveiling ceremony at the Ann Arbor campus.*

The University of Mankato's "Northern Light" had a unique design based on a solar array hinged down the middle so the team could face it towards the sun no matter which side of the car it was on. It gave their car a lot of versatility. Even still, every time the car was stuck behind traffic, the team wished it could fly!

Sunraycer with side pods which house four bicycle tires. Actually, the Sunrunner resembles an inverted horseshoe. The car body, three blended airfoils (one horizontal and two vertical), maximizes solar panel surface area and minimizes frontal area. This design allows for 50 percent more surface area for the solar cells mounted on the sides and on top of the body.

Another of Sunrunner's unique features is the dual motor system, with one motor connected to each rear wheel. One motor propels the car, while a second booster motor provides extra power for acceleration and hill climbing.

The University of Michigan demonstrated that efficiency in motion applies to human endeavors as well as automotive design. Fancy's able leadership was the catalyst and the fuel to keep the team on track. By the time they arrived in Orlando, this group was a well-oiled machine moving forward with tremendous momentum. They had tested and retested their car and studied every inch of the race route. They had arranged for a satellite uplink to gain meteorological information. And they had spares for every single part of their vehicle.

Although the student drivers knew they could coax the Sunrunner to cruise at 55 mph (88 kph), they were aiming at an average speed of 45 mph (56 kph). The team motto sums up their thinking for the 11-day race, "Slower is faster." Like Susan Fancy's controlled, calculated smile that unfolds slowly but steadily, the Sunrunner demonstrated what the turtle and hare learned long ago in their own

infamous competition, "Slow and steady ... and you surely know the rest!"

As each of the teams poured energy into its solar car enterprise, the momentum grew into a national showcase of can-do attitudes and state-of-the-art technology. From the Adirondacks to the Rockies, from the Florida coast to the California surf, 32 teams of optimistic college students tackled a project of immense proportions. This saga of "Sunracing" highlights the story of a few of these explorers.

Thirty-two teams ranging in size from 10 to 140 rode on sunbeams with the "race for the future." Each team was sure they had discovered the best approach. Each team was certain they had chosen winning advantages. Each team was filled with a burgeoning sense of accomplishment as they delivered the goods they had promised - 32 vehicles for the SUNRAYCE starting line.

In July 1990, teams unveiled their sun-seeking machines in one of the most awesome displays ever recorded in automotive history. Although the appearance of the students was not unusual, their vehicles ranked high in evoking stares of disbelief.

Among themselves, teams whispered, "Believe it or not, we made it!" After a year and a half of ups and downs, here they were to celebrate their own outstanding achievement with good old July sunshine. The temperature was high, but the emotions were even higher.

One of the most stunning sights in solar car racing is the panorama of all the cars together charging their batteries from the sun. This photo was taken the morning of the second day of GM SUNRAYCE USA in Floral Park, Florida.

The University of Maryland's "Pride of Maryland" (left) and Mankato State University's "Northern Light" prepare for the start of GM SUNRAYCE USA at the EPCOT Center in Orlando, Florida on July 9, 1990.

The dazzling start of GM SUNRAYCE USA included trumpets blaring and plenty of flags flying in the July sun. On the podium Robert Stempel, then president of General Motors, prepares to drop the green flag signaling the drivers of the solar cars to start their rays!

V. GM SUNRAYCE USA

What happened next is an unfolding of excitement, anxiety, suspense, and a special blend of competitive fun. Since very few of the team members had ever participated in a solar car race before, this was a whole new experience for most. The scene resembled an unrehearsed performance with a cast of characters not fully prepared for their roles.

One unifying element seemed apparent among the groups which arrived in Lake Buena Vista, Florida in July 1990. Each team shared a common point of view as they got ready to race: they could win. They wondered how their cars would perform on the road, but they dared not let any worries dampen their enthusiasm. As it turned out, this sure-fire optimism served the participants well throughout the SUNRAYCE. The 11-day event which was about to begin was filled with more than its share of ups and downs. The newness of the idea, the unpredictable nature of the elements involved, and the spectrum of personalities included made the SUNRAYCE a one-of-a-kind adventure.

What better place that the EPCOT Center for the SUNRAYCE starting line? Representing Walt Disney's vision of the world to come, EPCOT was built to be a blueprint for life in the future. Disney believed that advanced technology would help us make better use of Earth's resources to improve the quality of our lives.

A showcase of innovative prototype systems, the EPCOT Center seemed a likely place to begin SUNRAYCE. Just as the engineers who built the glistening Spaceship Earth (the world's largest geodesic sphere) faced many challenges, so did the teams who built the nation's first solar electric vehicles. EPCOT's developers were determined to create a unique glimpse of tomorrow's world; so were the students who committed themselves to SUNRAYCE. They were reaching into the future for solutions to today's problems.

Representatives from General Motors, the U.S Department of Energy, and the Society of Automotive Engineers were on hand to start the race. They were just as excited as the student teams, anxiously waiting for these space-age autos to be off and running. Although they were not competing, the participation of these individuals was equally vital. From official observers to

The media came out in throngs to catch the moment. As shown above, most lined up right across from the starting line.

pre-race scrutineers to data recorders, they helped make SUNRAYCE a success.

Pre-race scrutineering, safety inspections, and time trials were required of all teams before the official start of the SUNRAYCE. Teams were advised to appear with their cars at the Daytona International Speedway on July 6 to qualify for pole positions. All morning long twenty stock cars had thundered around the track. The deafening roar of their engines made spoken communication nearly impossible.

Then, at two o'clock, the solar cars had the track. Suddenly, there was silence. The high-pitched whine of the electric motors was audible down on the track, but not a sound was heard in the stands as the solar cars slid around the speedway. They slipped around the race track like silent creatures from another world.

Such an incredible contrast led some to fear that this race might be boring. Would it hold the attention of the curious crowd without the roaring vibrations? These fears soon disappeared. As the announcer reported standings and interviewed drivers, his voice resounded clearly over the track. As the cars stretched out down below, there were no exhaust emissions rising up to the crowd. Without the noise and fumes, these vehicles captured the spectators' undivided attention. They were witness to a silent revolution in auto racing. Instead of a race filled with loud noise and dangerous speeds, here was a competition of intellectual engineering with some good clean fun thrown in.

Jerry Williams, SUNRAYCE Program Manager, was in charge of the qualifying events. Capturing the nation's attention and spirit meant showcasing cars that were safe, roadworthy, and reasonably competitive. All 32 vehicles had to meet the following requirements to qualify for SUNRAYCE 1990:

- Maximum vehicle dimensions of 6 meters (19.7 feet) long by 2 meters (6.6 feet) wide by 1.6 meters (5.3 feet) high. Minimum height 1 meter (3.3 feet).
- Powered by sunlight with no more than 5 kilowatt-hours of battery capacity.
- Solar array not to exceed 4 meters (13.1 feet) long by 2 meters (6.6 feet) wide by 1.6 meters (5.3 feet) high. [Approximately 8 square meters.]
- Safety equipment to include adequate brakes, horns, turn indicators, windshield wipers, rear vision system, and seat belts.
- Tilt test to make sure wheels could turn corners safely.
- Driver exit test to ensure driver could get out of vehicle in 15 seconds or less.

All cars qualified for the race, although some failed on the first attempt and had to make immediate repairs and adjustments to pass inspection. Teams that were not ready learned a valuable lesson of racing: being prepared saves valuable time, effort, and anxiety. Observers wondered if the cars' scrutineering performance would be indicative of final race results. Unspoken predictions were being cal-

Time trials for starting grid positions took place at the Daytona 500 race track. The University of Michigan's "Sunrunner" (above) started in the number two position, qualifying with a clocked speed of 45 mph.

culated, but it was anyone's guess as to what would actually happen once the race began.

In addition to being inspected, the solar cars had to compete for pole position. The .5 kilometer slalom course consisted of eight cones spaced from 40 to 75 feet apart (12 to 23 meters) and a 1,050 foot (320 meter) straightaway. Once through the speed trap, cars had to come to a complete stop within a required distance. Starting positions were determined based on the total amount of time taken for each vehicle to drive the entire course. The car with the quickest time was awarded the pole position for day one of racing.

University of Maryland's "Pride" captured that coveted prize with a qualifying time of 44.46 seconds. The Pride was also the fastest car, timed at 52 mph (84 kph) on the straightaway. The team was elated, garnering immediate respect from competitors. The bright yellow Sunrunner from the University of Michigan was in second place with a recorded time of 45.77 seconds. The entry from Mankato State,

the Northern Light, was placed third with a time of 55.43 seconds. Teams had chosen numbers for their cars back in April 1989 when names were drawn out of a hat. Who would have guessed that Maryland's choice of number one, Michigan's number two, and Mankato's number three would have matched their starting positions 15 months later? An amazing coincidence!

Unfortunately, the bright sunshine which graced the early afternoon event at the Daytona Speedway turned into a merciless thunderstorm. Within moments, the track became a swollen river, and the solar cars were drenched in the downpour. Qualifications were suspended until the next day, when mother nature proved to be more cooperative. The remaining cars were inspected and tested near the EPCOT Center. Cal State L.A.'s Solar Eagle had an impressive showing with a qualifying time of 56.34 seconds and a top recorded speed of 49 mph. Maybe this was the car to beat.

TABLE 2: GM SUNRAYCE USA OFFICIAL QUALIFYING RESULTS

July 6, 7, & 8, 1990 (In sequence over four days of qualifying)

DAY	POS.	SCHOOL NAME	TEAM NAME	TEAM NO.	QUALIFYING ELPSD.TIME	PENALTY TIME	OFFICIAL QUAL.TIME	TRAP SPEED (m.p.h.)
1	1	Maryland	Pride of Maryland	1	0:44.46	0:00.00	0:44.46	52
	2	Michigan	Sunrunner	2	0:45.77	0:00.00	0:45.77	45
	3	Mankato	Northern Light	3	0:53.43	0:02.00	0:55.43	36
	4	Cal State LA	Solar Eagle	19	0:56.34	0:00.00	0:56.34	49
	5	UPRM	The Shining Star	92	1:06.33	0:00.00	1:06.33	38
	6	WMU/Jordan	Sunseeker	77	1:21.38	0:00.00	1:21.38	23
2	7	Cal Poly SLO	Sun Luis	101	0:35.86	0:00.00	0:35.86	49
	8	Virginia Tech	VT SOLARAY	6	0:42.24	0:00.00	0:42.24	37
	9	Stark	SolisTyrannus Cognocis	22	0:46.32	0:00.00	0:46.32	39
	10	Stanford	SUnSUrfer	100	0:46.72	0:00.00	0:46.72	36
	11	WWU	Viking XX	XX	0:49.11	0:00.00	0:49.11	33
	12	UNT	Centennial	8	0:49.70	0:00.00	0:49.70	23
	13	Waterloo	Midnight Sun	24	0:52.83	0:00.00	0:52.83	39
	14	Clarkson	Kalahkwaneha	4	0:55.33	0:00.00	0:55.33	28
	15	Drexel	SunDragon	76	0:58.21	0:00.00	0:58.21	33
	16	WPI	Starduster	90	0:59.14	0:02.00	1:01.14	48
	17	RIT	Spirit	10	1:04.24	0:00.00	1:04.24	29
	18	Cal Poly Pomona	Solar Flair	25	1:04.50	0:00.00	1:04.50	18
	19	Rose-Hulman	Solar Phantom	74	1:06.45	0:00.00	1:06.45	17
	20	Auburn	Sol of Auburn	11	1:10.53	0:00.00	1:10.53	19
	21	Crowder	Star II	33	1:16.06	0:00.00	1:16.06	28
3	22	Villanova	Wild Solarcat	111	0:45.08	0:00.00	0:45.08	33
	23	CSU	Stelar V	61	0:45.41	0:00.00	0:45.41	35
	24	MIT	Galaxy	5	0:51.74	0:00.00	0:51.74	27
	25	Dartmouth	Sunvox III	96	0:59.08	0:00.00	0:59.08	22
	26	Cal St. Northridge	CSUN-Blazer	0	1:04.61	0:00.00	1:04.61	19
	27	Ottawa	Team Ralos	37	1:12.73	0:00.00	1:12.73	23
	28	FIT	Sunshine Special	26	1:18.35	0:00.00	1:18.35	29
	29	Penn	Solsation	250	1:23.39	0:00.00	1:23.39	19
	30	Texas	Texas Native Sun	36	1:29.22	0:00.00	1:29.22	22
	31	Iowa	PriSUm	9	1:24.03	0:00.00	1:24.03	22
4	32	ASU	Sun Devil Cruiser	7	Qualified on July 9, 1990			

Qualifying at Daytona was interrupted when a thunderstorm made everyone scurry for cover. Shown here is the team from Clarkson University caught on the track as the downpour began.

July 9 finally arrived. Thirty-two teams of sun-loving racers lined up outside the gates of the EPCOT Center. They were about to prove that humans CAN travel from place to place in pollution-free cars, all on a tankful of sunshine. In an unusual array of color and sparkle, the gleaming solar vehicles showed no hint of anxiety. Their soulmates, the students who had toiled over them for a whole year, silently wished themselves good luck as they beamed at clicking cameras which promised to preserve a priceless memory on film. The weather joined in the celebration, as sunshine poured down upon the cars to brighten the day's festivities.

Disney lent musical talent to the event with an enthusiastic marching band. Everyone's beloved Mickey Mouse shared the limelight with GM President Robert Stempel. As they stepped up to the podium, a huge GM SUNRAYCE USA banner flew above their heads. Crisp white T-shirts with the familiar SUNRAYCE logo adorned dozens of people in the cheering crowd. The mixture of excitement and curiosity created a special feeling for the spectators and for the participants. Dreams of tomorrow's automotive technology touched reality as the race for the future began.

As the green flag went down to signal the start of the SUNRAYCE car number one, the Pride of Maryland, took off like a winner. Everyone assumed that being first was a distinct advantage, but Maryland's experience proved that assumption dead wrong. Less than one minute after taking off the Maryland team made a wrong turn. With no one up front to follow, the team did not realize the error until ten minutes later.

Bill Raynor, who was in charge of navigation, communicated his distress when he radioed from the lead vehicle, "We're going the wrong way." Team leader Larry Long was unconvinced and suggested that they continue. Eventually, they recognized the mistake and turned around to head back to the starting line. One wrong turn had cost them 36 minutes of precious racing time. The excitement of being first was transformed into dismay as Maryland started all over again. Instead of living up to the car's namesake, Pride, the students were embarrassed to end up behind all the other solar cars. Topping off their problems, the team had driven as fast as they could to get back to the EPCOT Center, using

Actually, many of the student-designed solar cars were not ready to go full speed ahead at the time of scrutineering. Last-minute repairs were a common denominator for nearly half of the registered teams. SUNRAYCE officials continued pre-race testing through the weekend until all vehicles were deemed ready to start. The figures listed in Table 2 are ordered according to the date that each car qualified. Teams that were ready went first. Those that were not had to wait, sacrificing the opportunity to take off from the starting line in one of the prized first positions.

At 11:00 am on July 9, 1990, the University of Maryland's "Pride of Maryland" (left) was given the green flag to start the GM SUNRAYCE USA.

up a lot of battery power. This was definitely not a great beginning for the Maryland team.

The performance of the Stelar V from Colorado State University was typical of the unpredictable nature of this race. Colorado's team came to Florida with a very unusual vehicle and very high spirits. Their solar cells were stacked in a triangular configuration to eke out more solar power from a fixed area. The tilting array could also track the sun. A computer inside the car made it possible for the array's angle to be adjusted automatically during any given day of driving. Despite its rather heavy weight, this vehicle had plenty of get-up-and-go.

Like many other vehicles, however, the Stelar V needed some finishing touches before the qualifying events. Not until the third day of scrutineering did the Stelar V show its stripes. Placed in twenty-third position to start the race, the Colorado students knew they had to come from behind. But they had lots of confidence. Mechanical engineer Jan Mickelson claimed their car had lots of "pep" and would scoot out front in no time.

By the close of day one, the Stelar V had lived up to the team's expectations. The Colorado car had moved up into fourth place, finishing three minutes ahead of the Michigan car (which had started off from EPCOT in second position). The team felt their rowdy cheers were well-deserved.

The first car to pull into Floral City, the designated destination for day one, was Cal State's Solar Eagle. The L.A. team had driven the 75 miles (121 km) in two hours and four minutes. Observers wondered if this car would have consistently high performance throughout the race. Team members thought so!

The sleek-looking Midnight Sun from the University of Waterloo in Canada finished second.

Although Colorado State University's "Stelar V" team started the race in 23rd position, they performed well and moved up to finish the first day's leg in 4th place.

The team was elated about the change in their position from thirteen to two. M.I.T.'s Galaxy also performed well, passing twenty solar cars that day to move into third place, just one minute behind the Midnight Sun. Worden was not surprised though, because he had designed the ultra-lightweight Galaxy for speed on the open road.

The Viking XX from Western Washington had a relatively smooth first day with plenty of power for covering the short distance. If not for a flat tire which took more than five costly minutes to repair, the car would have been in third position. Faculty advisor Michael Seal predicted an even better performance on day two. The team was pleased to move up from eleventh to sixth place, a mere thirty-six seconds behind Michigan's Sunrunner.

The Sunrunner cruised along steadily at a pre-calculated speed on the first day. Fancy's strategy of maintaining consistent speed was meant to prevent the unnecessary use of bat-

Cal State LA's "Solar Eagle" was the first car to cross the finish line in Floral Park, Florida, during the first day of the GM SUNRAYCE USA.

Crowder College's "Star II" on the road racing.

tery power. Although the Sunrunner had the power to drive faster, it was "too risky" to sprint ahead, leaving no reserve energy for cloudy days.

For the Cal Poly Pomona Solar Energy Team (CAPSET), the start of the race was a disappointment. Considered a pre-race favorite, the Solar Flair had a grueling first day. After driving a short distance, everything seemed to go wrong. The right front tire fell off. Then, the gears had to be changed when the car failed to make it up a hill. By mid-day, the motor controller had burned out. Later, the motor itself burned out. How the team maintained its optimistic spirit is a puzzlement.

One team that surprised everyone was Clarkson University. Their car, the Kalahkwaneha, sprinted from the starting line and performed well for the first 20 miles. The letdown came when the team realized the car was using up much more battery power than expected. After inspecting their array, they discovered several cracked solar cells. Deciding to make the necessary repairs immediately, they refused to let one day's frustrations dampen their soaring spirits. This dedicated bunch worked on their car until 8:30 that evening. They were unwilling to let a second-rate performance persist for the Kalahkwaneha. Believe it or not, the team was still smiling when they pulled into Floral City. Judging from their enthusiasm, spectators might have thought Clarkson was in first place rather than twenty-eighth.

Day one of SUNRAYCE came to a memorable close with a dinner of country cooking for the 32 solar car teams. Although they were certainly hungry for food, the students were even hungrier for stories about what had happened on the open road. Everyone had a tale to tell. The "unexpected" had occurred more often than not, and teams shared a special comraderie as they exchanged racing epithets.

As planned by General Motors and the Department of Energy, the daily awards ceremony coincided with dinner. Teams who finished in first, second, and third place for the day were recognized and presented with T-shirts and commemorative pins. Race officials and observers also chose two teams to be honored for their outstanding display of sportsmanship and teamwork on each day of racing. The teams from Michigan and Maryland received these honors on day one.

The University of Michigan had offered their "machine shop" (in the back of their truck) to other schools and provided several electronic components to their arch-competitor, the University of Maryland. They were the recipients of the sportsmanship award. The Maryland team received the teamwork award, in recognition of the rational and professional manner in which they handled the "wrong turn" situation at the start of the race.

At the dinner, Mr. Wilbur Langley, Commissioner of Citrus County, Florida, presented a resolution to SUNRAYCE sponsors and students to commemorate the SUNRAYCE. Citrus County was very proud to host the racers. He congratulated all the participants on their achievement and dedication to the betterment of education and the environment.

Following the dinner and awards ceremony, teams held final planning meetings to prepare their strategies for day two. Afterward, they retired to a variety of accommodations, some camping out near their solar cars in the parking lot and some staying together in nearby hotel rooms. Most of them were up till midnight. They knew sunrise would follow a short six hours later. That left little time for sleep because their solar panels would need to be up for charging by no later than 7 AM. This was literally a race against time.

At dawn on July 10, the hillside at Floral City was an awesome scene of tilted solar arrays and electric motors exposed to the open air. Students finished final engine checks and recharged their cars' batteries in the bright morning sunlight. Fortunately, mother nature was on their side, blessing them with solar rays unimpeded by cloud cover.

The reality of "sunracing" was more apparent on this second day. That early common denominator of euphoria was transformed into hard-core practicality. The business of solar racing was not a mindless game, but an intellectual and physical pursuit. In Tholstrup's words, the "brain sport" was on.

The local media turned out in full force with radio, television, and newspaper journalists on hand to capture unique stories and photographs. Students found themselves catapulted into the limelight as reporters hovered over their vehicles. Hundreds of spectators joined the media in circulating among the teams, reaching out to touch these seemingly unreal creations which decorated the lawn so proudly. Everyone wanted to know all about the cars and how they had come into being. The deluge of questions ranged from, "How fast do they go?" to "How much do they cost?"

Barely recovered from lack of sleep and the over stimulation of the past few days, the students were more tense as they began the second day of serious competition. This day's driving through Florida's panhandle would be twice as far. On top of that, the July weather was a merciless combination of heat and humidity. Even T-shirts and shorts seemed way too much apparel for bodily comfort.

When the cars took off at 9 AM, it was anyone's guess which ones would arrive in Tallahassee first. The surprising series of experiences on day one made the very idea of predicting winners seem ludicrous. Perhaps this was what made SUNRAYCE so exciting. Just as the weather often refuses to comply with meteorologists' forecasts, so the solar car competition resisted predictability.

Over the next ten days SUNRAYCE teams became well-acquainted with the highs and lows of solar racing. There was plenty of excite-

Crowder's "Star II" is tilted toward the sun to help recharge its batteries on the morning of the second day in Floral City, Florida.

Each day the solar cars had to stop at a mid-day stop which is one of the best places to see the race teams and their solar cars. Shown above is Crowder's "Star II" at the mid-day stop in Dothan, Alabama on the third day of the race.

192 miles (309 km) of pavement from Floral City to Tallahassee. Each team cruised silently as it maneuvered for its place in the sun and on the road. At the midday public stop, the Department of Energy ran out of the daily allotment of 1,000 programs in no time, with visitors clamoring for more information about these "sun-guzzlers." By now, local news stations as well as national broadcasting networks were covering the SUNRAYCE story. And all along the route enthusiastic crowds bolstered the spirits of SUNRAYCE teams. These people were more than curious; they were genuinely interested in the solar cars. "What kind of magic do those solar cells contain to power a moving vehicle?" they inquired.

For Michigan driver Paula Finnegan, the second day's public stop offered a surprising experience. When she pulled in, she heard loud applause and wondered what had happened. As she climbed out of the Sunrunner, the cheers grew louder and louder. Suddenly, she realized they were applauding for her! Overwhelmed by the spectators' enthusiasm, she was soon signing autographs. Finnegan lost all track of time. It was team leader Susan Fancy who reminded her that the ten-minute break was over. In this race, every second counted.

Other drivers later shared similar stories of "celebrity status" at the public stops. Anyone with doubts about the market for solar electric vehicles would have been easily dissuaded by these scenes.

ment as they traveled the 1,644 miles (2,645 km) from Florida to Michigan. But unexpected challenges also meant plenty of difficulty along the way. Since no two teams or cars were alike, the responses to the hard work, fun, and adversity were unique. Like seeds sown in the wind, the outcome was unknown.

On day two of SUNRAYCE the solar cars stretched out under the hot July sun along the

Stanford's "SUnSUrfer" being given the signal to continue racing after their 10-minute mid-day stop.

A glimpse at the next ten days tells a story of intense activity. Although there were frustrations for all, most SUNRAYCE teams experienced firsthand the many dimensions of success. A few highlights reveal the special character of this race for the future.

FRIDAY THE THIRTEENTH

On the fifth day of racing, mother nature reinforced what some feared Friday the thirteenth might bring. Teams were greeted by a sky full of ominous-looking rain clouds on that morning in Haleyville, Alabama. Heavy rain the night before had turned the ground into a sea of brown mud. To top it off, the weather report called for continued thunderstorms throughout the day.

For the team from Worcester Polytechnic Institute (WPI), however, day five was a lucky one. Feeling somewhat discouraged by poor standings after four days of racing, the team was determined to see the "Starduster" in a winning position. Advisors Edward Clark and Roy Richard knew their car had lots of power, and they knew their students needed a boost. WPI chose a bold strategy. They would drive the Starduster as fast as they could until they moved up to the front of the pack.

Surprisingly, the plan worked. By midday they had passed the frontrunners, trouncing the Viking XX by 90 minutes and the Sunrunner by two hours! They even managed to catch three hours of partial sun after breaking free of the thickest storm clouds. The Starduster had covered the 140-mile trip in less than seven hours, by far the best performance of the day. By day's end, WPI's first place finish had improved their overall standings from 23rd to 14th position. After that, competitors referred to their car as the "Worcester Rocket."

GM President Robert Stempel beamed with pride as he presented the WPI team with their award that evening. A 1955 graduate of Worcester Polytechnic Institute, Stempel was delighted to bestow the honors on his alma mater. Standing by the podium at GM's new Saturn plant in Spring Hill Tennessee, team leader Brian Glatz grinned from ear to ear. The Starduster had finally shown its stripes. That moment provided just the right dose of adrenalin for a team that had not yet tasted success. And for other teams whose cars had not performed so well during the first half of the race, this come-from-behind victory became a shot of self-confidence. If WPI could take first place, so could they!

University of Michigan's "Sunrunner" (above) pulls into an overnight stop in Mason, Michigan.

University of Maryland team member Tracy Styslinger being interviewed during GM SUNRAYCE USA.

CHURCHILL DOWNS

For teams jockeying for position at the front of the pack, Saturday, July 15 proved to be an exciting day. The skies had cleared and bright sunlight was pouring down on the SUNRAYCE cars. Most of the cars were now running in top condition, and the drivers had a better feel for the competition. With plenty of sunshine, many felt they could make up time, so the pace quickened, too. Broad smiles were the order of the day as they took off from Louisville, Kentucky in positive spirits.

As they neared the end of this seventh day, the frontrunners struggled for that prized first-place finish. The Sunrunner was ahead most of the morning, but MIT's Galaxy and WWI's Viking XX pulled into the midday public stop only one minute behind the Michigan team. Later, as they drove into Louisville, the Galaxy was right on the Sunrunner's tail. The narrow, congested streets in town prevented the MIT driver from passing Michigan, but he was determined to make the challenge. As they approached the Churchill Downs parking lot (that day's stopping point), the finish line appeared 200 yards in front of them. Suddenly, the Galaxy accelerated. Shocked into action, the Sunrunner responded by zooming forward. It was a rare treat for the spectators to witness the photo-finish of this unanticipated two-car contest. As it turned out, the Sunrunner crossed the line only a half car-length ahead of the Galaxy!

ON TO INDIANAPOLIS

July 16 dawned with plenty of sunshine, but this day's distance was greater and there was one major hill to climb. Amazing as it seemed, the team from Clarkson University was still optimistic about the race. The "Kalahkwaneha" had finished near the bottom of the heap for seven consecutive days and had more than its share of breakdowns along the route. Up to now the Clarkson team had been unable to reach any of the midday public stops. Undaunted, they were more determined than ever to make it.

Monday's pit stop was located near the Ohio River. The race route included a steep downhill slope approaching the bridge to cross the river. Just two miles from the hill, the Kalahkwaneha's batteries were desperately low. Driver Joe Capraro called out the battery voltage, "85 volts, 70, 60...." Could they make it to the hill before the batteries went dead?

The Clarkson team refused to give up hope despite their dire predicament. Then, looming in front of them like a mirage was a sign that read, "TRUCKS USE LOW GEAR." As they began to pick up speed the team praised everything they could think of! Now they were certain they would make it. The car crossed over the bridge, pulling into the public stop to the sound of exuberant cheers. There was "high-fiving" in every direction. The panoramic view by the river seemed a perfect backdrop for the unexpected excitement. It was a day this team would never forget!

From the public stop the route continued on toward Indianapolis, leaving the Ohio River Valley. Just outside of Madison, Indiana was the longest, steepest hill of the entire race route. It was 1.8 miles (2.9 km) in length with a steady 10 percent grade. "Why not have a hill climb competition?" suggested Hans Tholstrup and Urs Muntwyler, who were both traveling with the race. It was unanimously accepted, so Tholstrup positioned himself at the bottom, and Muntwyler was stationed at the top. As the solar cars passed by, they clicked their stopwatches to see which car could climb the fastest.

What a thrill it was for the WPI team! Their Starduster mustered the power to ascend the hill 37 seconds faster than any other car. Maryland's Pride came in second, with Crowder's Star II clocking in a close third.

For the experienced, diligent group from Crowder, SUNRAYCE represented an opportunity to surpass their earlier achievements with solar vehicles. The Star II, which team leader Steve Tipton called a "labor of love," was performing well in this race, maintaining a fifth-place position by day ten. But the car had not yet had a first-place finish. On July 18 the team decided to forego their more conservative strategy of relatively consistent speed on the road. This was the last full day of racing, and they were only 90 minutes behind the third place team. The Crowder students realized that the winner's circle was still within their grasp, and they were not about to let it slip away.

Everything seemed right for an extra push forward, and the team rallied for an unprecedented display of energy and spirit. As the Star II began the 190-mile (306-km) leg of the route, Art Boyt flashed his characteristic broad smile at the driver. This day would be different. Starting off in sixth place, the Star II soon passed every solar car ahead of it. In fact,

Left: WPI winning the hill climb competition.

GM SUNRAYCE USA was an 11-day cross-country race that took the teams through parts of the country most of the students had never seen before. Sometimes hundreds of people would line the streets such as those watching the Maryland team from the bridge (above). Other times they travelled alone or they might just have to sit by the side of the road while team members fixed a breakdown. Shown below is the Maryland team sitting by the road just outside of Nashville, Tennessee.

the Crowder team was so determined to excel that they never looked back. The bright sunshine beckoned them to beat all odds and go for it. When they crossed under the checkered flag at the finish line in Mason, Michigan in first place for the day, the Crowder team was awash with hugs and handshakes.

Like a dream come true, the Crowder first-place finish delivered a surge of excitement to this team that had worked so hard. With only 84 miles (135 km) left in the final stretch to Warren, Michigan, the Star II and its drivers were raring to go. Their steadfast determination was transformed into a gallant attempt to outdo all the competition on the road. Nothing could stop them now!

TOUGH CHALLENGES

THE SOLAR FLAIR'S DIFFICULTIES

By day three the Pomona team had become accustomed to repairing their car on the fly. Kathy Payne toiled away on the new solar array. Even though it was only two-thirds complete, she found it was capable of producing more power than the old array. The team decided to install the new panel and saw an immediate improvement in the car's performance. This change eventually allowed Pomona to move up from fifteenth to eighth place, a surprise to all.

Meanwhile, Payne continued to work on the array in the evening until it was finally finished. For the next few days, the Solar Flair would pull in at day's end and she would begin working. Amazing as it seemed, the Pomona team refused to get discouraged. A hefty dose of self-confidence and hope kept them going in an upbeat mood.

THE TEXAS NATIVE SUN

Another team which faced nearly insurmountable trouble was the University of Texas (Austin). By day five the rainy weather had created serious problems for the solar array. The cells were not sealed well enough to keep the water out, and the car lost power every time it rained. The team had fallen back to twenty-sixth place and was almost ready to give up. Feeling tired and dejected, some wanted to go home. Fortunately, at least half the team felt a strong commitment to finishing SUNRAYCE. After all, they had spent months preparing for this experience and they were unwilling to give up.

On the morning of July 13, that notoriously unlucky date, the Texas Native Sun was losing power despite the team's attempts to dry out the array. They decided to pull the car over behind a bank in the small town of Loretto, Tennessee, where they could put the array under the roof over the drive-up window to do their repair work.

As the team applied more sealant between the solar cells, their activity began to attract the local residents. Soon, throngs of local residents were standing all around. They were curious and wanted to know how they could help. One man even offered some drying lamps. Slowly but surely the car was put back into racing condition. It was quite a spectacle to see the students working side-by-side with the townspeople. The sense of togetherness brought the frustrated UT team back into focus. By midday, the car was ready to roll again. If not for the friendly assistance of the folks from Loretto, the Texas Native Sun might never have stayed in the SUNRAYCE. As it was, their interest and enthusiasm helped the UT team muster the perseverance to keep pushing on.

THE CANADIAN TEAMS

The two Canadian entries in the SUNRAYCE had garnered respect and friendship from all their competitors. The Midnight Sun from the University of Waterloo had seemed like the team to beat on the first day of racing. Bursting out of the starting line, the Midnight Sun came in second on day one. But they had worn down their batteries and could not recharge when the weather turned cloudy the following day. On the second day they were driving solely on solar energy and had no reserve power. The team fell back into sixteenth place because of their miscalculated strategy.

The other Canadian team, Team Ralos from the University of Ottawa, experienced persistent mechanical and motor problems from the beginning of SUNRAYCE. Despite the fact that they were almost always at the back of the pack, this team never let disappointment crush their determination.

On July 17 they decided to let nothing keep them from traveling the entire distance before the official stopping time at 6:30 PM. During the last half-hour they were actually counting the minutes. Finally they saw the Darke County Fairgrounds, the day's end in Greenville, Ohio. With only 20 seconds to spare, the driver floored the accelerator and zoomed across the finish line. The thunderous applause showed how much support this team had earned. One of the highlights of SUNRAYCE was watching this last-place team come cruising in to victory. All of Canada would have burst with pride at the sight.

MIT'S MISFORTUNE

On that same day, MIT's Galaxy had a breakdown which ultimately cost the team their second-place position in SUNRAYCE. The Galaxy had performed remarkably well for eight consecutive days, and MIT had a comfortable hold on a front runner's spot. On the way from Indianapolis to Greenville, however, misfortune took over. The Galaxy's front shock broke just before the team reached the midday stop point in Anderson, Indiana. Since they did not have a spare shock, they rigged the car to make it as far as the public stop. James Worden then began calling local auto parts stores in an attempt to find what they needed. When he had no success, he started calling all the local junk yards.

After what seemed like an eternity to the MIT team, Worden located a junk yard that had a used motorcycle shock which might fit. Unfortunately, the place was a half-hour away, and Worden had only vague directions on how to get there. They knew their slim four-hour lead on Maryland's Pride was now in jeopardy. MIT's team was a collection of grim-looking faces. As luck would have it, a local resident had overheard their dilemma and offered to drive Worden to retrieve the part.

Five hours later the Galaxy was repaired and back on the road. Had it not been for the helpful fellow from Anderson, it might have been eight hours later. As it was, MIT fell behind Maryland, moving down into sixth place overall. Lacking a necessary spare part

ended up being a costly error for this team. Like many of life's lessons, the MIT students learned this one the hard way.

The unbelievable turnout at the Anderson midday stop was a real boost to MIT at a time they needed it most. The spectators cheered and applauded wildly as each solar car pulled in, and many of them asked for team members' autographs. An announcer conducted live interviews and recognized every team that arrived with a note of tribute befitting heroes. A long line had formed near the DOE booth as people clamored to get SUNRAYCE programs. For anyone who questioned the significance of this race, the town of Anderson put those fears to rest.

EVENTS OF SPECIAL SIGNIFICANCE

SUNRAYCE was a unique experience filled with moments of special significance. Some of the most memorable events were thrilling, some awesome, and others heart-warming.

DREXEL PUPPY

The team from Drexel University was cruising along a rural road in Alabama on day three of the race when they nearly hit an abandoned puppy. The small brown-haired canine won their hearts instantly, and they decided to take it to a local veterinarian for a check-up. Once the puppy had its shots, the Drexel crew figured it was fit for racing. Their solar car was called the Sun Dragon, so they named the puppy SD2, short for "Sun Dragon Solar Dog."

WPI's "Starduster" arrives at the mid-day stop in the Applewood Shopping Center in Anderson, Indiana, which had the largest crowd during the 11-day race.

SD2 became the Drexel mascot and a beloved favorite of all the SUNRAYCE teams. For many, the puppy was symbolic. After all, this race was about preserving precious natural resources for all life on Earth. Here was a simple critter whose future depended upon us. SD2 left a lasting impression upon lots of folks and took center stage in a lot of photographs. The Solar Dog stayed with the Drexel team throughout the entire course of the race and eventually became a pet of one of the team members.

CLARKSON'S SPEEDING TICKET

On that same day, the Clarkson team had pulled over in the parking lot of an abandoned restaurant in Donaldsonville, Georgia.

Drexel named their car the "Sun Dragon" (top) and their mascot, "Sun Dragon Solar Dog," or "SD2" for short, shown (bottom) with Admiral James D. Watkins, Secretary of Energy.

The team was trying to recharge the Kalahkwaneha's batteries with what little sunlight was available. Before long the car was surrounded by a curious crowd of all ages. Happy for the attention at a discouraging moment, the Clarkson team promptly began giving children turns sitting behind the wheel of the solar car.

Proud parents were clicking away at camera shutters when a local policeman arrived on the scene to see what all the commotion was about. The Clarkson students persuaded him to give them a speeding ticket and a police patch. These were taped to the inside of the car's hood, the beginning of a tradition for the Kalahkwaneha. Clarkson collected insignia and "honorary" speeding tickets from almost every state through which they passed on the SUNRAYCE route.

CSU'S RAINY INTERVIEW

The severe thunderstorm that pelted the solar car teams on July 11 ended up on a positive note for the Colorado crew. Since the driver could not see well enough to drive, they had pulled the Stelar V off the roadway. Team members draped a large sheet of plastic over the entire car. They were sitting on the ground under the car's solar array holding onto the plastic. A few minutes later, a film crew from ESPN drove up and stopped next to them. Team captain Kip March motioned for the crew to join them under the car. And they did! It was the first time ESPN had conducted an interview underneath a solar car and the first time any of the solar car teams felt good about the rain!

INDIANAPOLIS SPEEDWAY

July 16 was a memorable day for every individual connected with the SUNRAYCE. Upon arrival in Indianapolis, the solar cars were to drive a lap around the famed Indianapolis Speedway. For the first time in its history, the Speedway would be used for an event other than the Indy 500.

Maryland team member Bill Raynor's comments capture the feelings of many on that historic afternoon. "From the time I was seven years old my dad and I watched the Indy races. He gave me an Indy patch when I was ten, which I wore on my jacket. Driving on the track today was like a dream come true. As we drove down the backstretch, tears of emotion welled up in my eyes. I will cherish that moment for the rest of my life."

Staring down at the Indy track while the solar car parade made its way around the

Speedway was an incredible experience. Silently, the 32 vehicles cruised side-by-side in a magnificent line-up of color and sparkle. Western Washington's Viking XX achieved the highest recorded speed of the SUNRAYCE when it was clocked at 54 mph (87 kph) on the straightaway there. This invalidated those assumptions that solar cars only go slowly!

THE GOVERNOR'S GREETINGS

On the tenth day of racing, the teams were on the last stretch in Michigan, the state to host the SUNRAYCE finale. It was only fitting that Michigan's Sunrunner was in first place on home turf. At dinner that evening, Governor Blanchard came to congratulate all the teams and wish them well on their last day of racing. His excitement was evident, and he was delighted to have a chance to address the student teams.

A highlight of the race was the use of the Indianapolis Motor Speedway for part of the route. On the morning of the ninth day, the solar cars were lined up in their starting order. The front row (below, l-r) consisted of Western Washington's "Viking XX," Michigan's "Sunrunner" and Maryland's "Pride of Maryland."

The University of Maryland finished the eighth day in first place, so they had the honor of parking in the winner's circle at the Indianapolis Motor Speedway. Shown (above) sitting in the "Pride of Maryland" is driver Steve Brady.

Blanchard said he was very impressed with the students' efforts at building and racing photovoltaic cars. He was especially pleased to honor the team from Michigan whose yellow Sunrunner seemed destined for a stellar performance in the SUNRAYCE. The significance of having Michigan's governor recognize the potential of this new alternative to the internal combustion engine was clear. If America's automakers realized the possibilities for solar electric vehicles, then this race could make a real difference.

REWARDS OF SUNRAYCE

Perhaps some of the finer moments of SUNRAYCE were the times when ordinary people stood wide-eyed in amazement as the solar cars breezed by on the roads. Children, with their staunch belief in the power of the future, were a joy to behold as they cheered the passing cars.

One touching experience took place at the midday public stop in Dothan, Alabama on July 12. An elderly man came to see the cars with his daughter. As he stared at the SUN-RAYCE vehicles, he recalled watching one of the first horseless carriages drive through his hometown when he was a young boy. He remembered running down the street behind it, amazed at what he saw. When he heard about solar cars coming to town, the man said he insisted on seeing them. "I wouldn't have missed them," he said fondly. "What marvel will people think of next?"

The Viking XX from Western Washington University was by far one of the biggest attention-getters of SUNRAYCE. Its clever design with the huge tilted array and the two-person side pod always drew curious stares. The best scenes occurred at the midday pit stops. Here, the team would pick up the car and turn it around 180 degrees. The crowds loved watching it being lifted up and maneuvered into position the opposite way! They would wave to the driver facing backwards as the car sped off once again. Designed to travel in two directions to take advantage of the changing angles of the sun's rays throughout the day, the Viking was a clear example of ingenious creativity. No other entry in the competition matched this one in terms of uniqueness.

FINAL DAY OF RACING

Is there ever a safe lead in a race? The Michigan team had done well throughout SUNRAYCE, but Fancy kept reminding her team that races are not over until they are really over. An accident, a breakdown, or another team's shining performance could change everyone's status in short order.

Heavy thunderstorms the night before prevented battery recharging after the long 190-mile trip from Greenville, Ohio to Mason, Michigan. Although sunshine was plentiful the morning of July 19, most cars were starting out on very low batteries. This made the final leg of racing a true run on solar energy and resulted in a few surprises.

For the Crowder team, the excitement of a first-place win the day before was fresh in everyone's minds. As Steve Tipton and Tonya Props got into the Star II, they looked up to see the Goodyear Blimp overhead. Tipton told Art Boyt he couldn't wait to get started, and Boyt signaled with a thumbs up. Unfortunately, just after starting a motor chain came off and wedged itself between the sprocket and the wheel. The repairs cost them some precious time and prevented them from overtaking the front runners. They were delighted, however, to secure a fifth-place finish for the day and fifth place overall in the race. In fact, their car was one of the most consistent of all the entries, placing fifth or sixth almost every day of SUNRAYCE.

The WPI team decided to go all out on that final day. Starting in twenty-seventh position, driver Avi Klinger passed 22 cars in the first 50 miles! He vied for position with Crowder for several miles until they reached a hill. The Starduster outpowered the Star II on the incline and beat them to the finish line, minutes behind the front runners. Their fourth-place finish that day put them into fourteenth position overall for the race. A gallant try for this determined crew.

Nothing seemed to be easy for the CAPSET group from Pomona. The last day was no different. Their gear sprocket was worn down to a paper-thin spindle, but they were determined to make it to the end. They drove cautiously the last 84 miles and surprised themselves when they placed in the top ten. The team was ecstatic and relieved that their troubles were finally over.

The Solsation from the University of Pennsylvania was a miracle in itself. At some point during the race, every major component of the car had broken down. But every time, the team had managed to repair their car and get back on the road. The team seldom had a full night of sleep. Strengthened by their experiences, the team felt as if they could fix ANY-THING! After day three, they had placed a sign on the back of the Solsation which read,

"Caution: Frequent Breaking." Needless to say, they were relieved when the race was finally over.

Never able to compensate for the Galaxy's breakdown on day nine, the MIT team was holding onto its sixth place standing. Barely three hours behind Crowder's total elapsed time, Worden's crew buried their disappointment in the excitement of placing in the top ten. The Galaxy had shown consistent performance and had proved to be one of the fastest cars. The team finished the race feeling they had accomplished many of their objectives.

As they pulled out on their last day of racing, the Maryland team knew they were close to clinching third place. Their "Pride" had responded beautifully during the past eleven days, yet they felt it would have done even better if they had been more familiar with its workings. Crossing under the checkered flag second in line put Maryland in third place overall. Exhilarated and swelling with pride, the Maryland team let it all out with a rousing celebration.

Western Washington's Viking XX was one of the few vehicles that had plenty of battery power on this final day. Since they had not yet come in first on any of the previous legs of the journey, the WWU team decided to push to the limits on this one. They averaged 37 mph (60 kph) from Mason to Warren, Michigan. Arriving to the sound of wildly cheering crowds, they were finally the first car to drive past the checkered flag. What a spectacular way to end the

race! They placed second overall and had challenged the number one car, Michigan's Sunrunner, throughout the entire race.

The Sunrunner's team made their first strategical error on that final day. Driving fast at the start of the day, they soon drained the car's batteries (which had no reserve because of the previous evening's rain and cloudy weather) and had to drive slowly on solar power alone. To make matter worse, twenty miles from the finish line the drive chain broke off the primary motor, forcing them to push their car off the road for last-minute repairs. As other cars cruised by, the Michigan team felt the tension mounting. Once back on the road, they were caught in traffic "as thick as molasses." Then, when they were in sight of the finish line a train approached. Before the car crossed the tracks, the gates came down and they had to wait for the entire train to pass by. After what seemed like hours, they were on their way again. Team leader Susan Fancy called it the most intense morning she had ever had!

The Sunrunner's modest performance on the last day did not ruin their chances of victory, however. The commanding lead of this well-prepared team from the University of Michigan insured their first-place position overall, securing their place in history as the winner of the GM SUNRAYCE USA. As the Sunrunner crossed the finish line, a chorus of "Hail to the

Close behind the winning Michigan car was the gallant team from Western Washington University in their "Viking XX." Thousands were on hand to watch the finish at the GM Tech Center in Warren, Michigan.

Western Washington's team (above) in front of their Viking XX.

The University of Michigan was the first solar car team to reach the finish line (above) winning the 1990 GM SUNRAYCE USA. As the "Sunrunner" crossed the finish line, the entire team ran along behind it to share in the glory.

The Michigan students couldn't have been happier after winning the race. Team leader Susan Fancy (below) celebrates with her team.

In the winner's circle, the jubilant Michigan team (below) was given sunflowers, proudly displayed by Susan Fancy (far left) and team driver Paula Finnegan (left).

The winning team leaders holding their first, second, and third place trophies: Susan Fancy (center) from the University of Michigan (first place); Bill Lingenfelter (left) from Western Washington University (second place); and Larry Long (right) from the University of Maryland (third place).

TABLE 3: GM SUNRAYCE USA OFFICIAL FINAL RESULTS

POSITION	SCHOOL NAME	TEAM NAME	NUMBER	CUM. TIME*
1	Michigan	Sunrunner	2	72:50:47
2	WWU	Viking XX	XX	74:10:06
3	Maryland	Pride of Maryland	1	80:10:55
4	Cal State LA	Solar Eagle	19	81:03:44
5	Crowder	Star II	33	81:06:18
6	MIT	Galaxy	5	84:17:37
7	Stanford	SUnSUrfer	100	93:56:53
8	WMU/Jordan	Sunseeker	77	96:55:20
9	CSU	Stelar V	61	97:55:06
10	Cal Poly Pomona	Solar Flair	25	99:05:57
11	Drexel	SunDragon	76	100:03:40
12	RIT	Spirit	10	104:21:18
13	Stark	Solis Tyrannus Cognocis	22	105:06:47
14	WPI	Starduster	90	106:34:60
15	Auburn	Sol of Auburn	11	107:24:35
16	Mankato	Northern Light	3	108:18:45
17	Iowa State	PrISUm	9	109:08:29
18	North Texas	Centennial	8	110:48:04
19	Cal St. Northridge	CSUN-Blazer	0	110:49:57
20	Rose-Hulman	Solar Phantom	74	111:07:44
21	Cal Poly SLO	Sun Luis	101	113:00:15
22	Texas	Texas Native Sun	36	113:15:25
23	Dartmouth	Sunvox III	96	113:48:13
24	Waterloo	Midnight Sun	24	114:37:15
25	FIT	Sunshine Special	26	116:39:41
26	Penn	Solsation	250	122:14:48
27	Virginia Tech	VT SOLARAY	6	130:27:08
28	Clarkson	Kalahkwaneha	4	131:52:00
29	Ottawa	Team Ralos	37	132:48:19
30	UPRM	The Shining Star	92	135:44:30
31	ASU	Sun Devil Cruiser	7	135:49:18
32	Villanova	Wild Solarcat	111	137:04:11

* Hours:Minutes:Seconds

Victor" rang out from the crowd. Team members lifted a beaming Paula Finnegan out of the car for congratulatory hugs.

University of Michigan President James Duderstadt called up on the team's portable phone with hearty congratulations. He said the Sunrunner's performance "exemplified the Michigan spirit - the willingness to go all out and to be the very best." GM President Robert Stempel and Advanced Engineering Vice President Don Runkle were on hand for the celebration, looking mighty proud of all the students and their spectacular solar cars which had just traversed the country on super sunpower.

For the top three teams, the coveted prize was a trip to Australia to compete in the 1990 World Solar Challenge, just three months away. First-place Michigan, second-place Western Washington, and third-place Maryland were only at the beginning of their solar racing saga and had another challenge awaiting them. Fourth-place Cal State L.A., fifth-place Crowder, and tenth-place Pomona also decided to compete Down Under, so they had both engineering and fundraising preparations to take care of. November would beckon their cars to distant shores before they knew it!

CONCLUSION

The creators of SUNRAYCE envisioned a program for university students that would motivate them to undertake a complex, ambitious project and see it through to fruition. SUNRAYCE was a means of elevating scientific learning to its highest level. This project was not confined to the classroom but included hands-on experimenting and testing of real-world equipment and technology.

SUNRAYCE asked students to apply their creative thinking in a unique competition. What started out as a race among students ended up as a race among engineers and scientists. The lessons learned surpassed what SUNRAYCE developers had imagined. The program was an overwhelming success, and the end result was a legacy of inspiring achievement.

SUNRAYCE was the dawn of a new collegiate sport, a sport for both scientists and car enthusiasts. In the SUNRAYCE competition, racing was heightened to its highest level. Hopefully, SUNRAYCE will serve to focus more attention on aspiring engineers and scientists in our nation's universities. What a way to go!

This was the scene as thousands anxiously waited for the solar cars to reach the finish line at the GM Tech Center in Warren, Michigan.

DIVERSITY IN THE FIELD OF 1990 GM SUNRAYCE USA PARTICIPANTS

Iowa State University's "PrISUm."

Rose-Hulman Institute of Technology's "Solar Phantom."

Stark Technical College's "Solis Tyrannus Cognoscis."

Arizona State University's "Sun Devil Cruiser."

Dartmouth College's "Sunvox III."

Virginia Tech's "VT Solaray."

Florida Tech's "Sunshine Special."

The University of Puerto Rico's "The Shining Star."

Villanova University's "Wild Solarcat."

Australia is considered one of the last frontiers, a place where one can explore vast areas of unsettled territory. Australia is a big land, the world's largest island. The same size as the U.S. mainland, Australia is a place of striking contrasts: seemingly endless shoreline and huge interior deserts; majestic, breathtaking panoramas of fertile countryside and desolate, blistered, uninhabitable land.

The Australian interior seems almost immeasurable. The outback of Australia includes four great deserts and consists of nearly two million square kilometers of badlands. Travel across this hot, parched expanse of earth blurs one's sense of time and distance. This humbling environment quickly reveals how frail the human body is if caught unprepared.

Reference to the Outback is often romantic and idealized, yet this land is barely capable of sustaining life. Tourism and the addition of new roads have made the Outback more accessible, but very few Australians actually live there. This romanticized image of the last frontier is home to only a few thousand people. In fact, Australia is one of the most urban areas of the world, with more than 70% of its people living in the towns and cities along the coast. Fifty percent of the population live in Sidney and Melbourne, with less than 1% of the population living in the sprawling Northern Territory.

Hans Tholstrup, the creator of the World Solar Challenge, chose a route stretching south from Darwin to Adelaide. The famed Stuart Highway which connects these two cities dissects the continent, running straight through the center of the Outback. The World Solar Challenge route, over 3,000 kilometers (1,870 miles) long, provides one of the most challenging race tracks in the world.

The "Spirit of Biel" on the lonesome Stuart Highway during the first day of the 1990 World Solar Challenge.

VI. On to Australia: The Land Down Under

Cal Poly Pomona's "Solar Flair" and the most famous landmark in Australia, Ayres Rock, which rises majestically in the middle of the Outback.

Back in the United States there was little time to rest for the six SUN-RAYCE teams who were planning to race in Australia. The 1990 World Solar Challenge started on November 11, barely three months after the SUNRAYCE finish. The teams from Michigan, Western Washington, Maryland, Cal State L.A., Crowder and Pomona were soon back to work fine-tuning their cars and preparing for the journey to Australia. Still full of enthusiasm, the students were anxious for the next competitive adventure.

The Michigan crew knew their Sunrunner was a very reliable car, but they also knew that it was too heavy. They reduced the car's weight by 70 pounds (32 kgs) by using only one motor instead of carrying the backup booster motor used in SUNRAYCE. They also replaced much of their steel suspension with titanium.

Western Washington replaced the Viking's solar array with improved space grade cells. This change increased the car's total power output from 1,500 to 1,700 watts under sunny skies.

The team felt that having one of the most powerful arrays would help them win the race.

The Maryland team focused their attention on improving the Pride's reliability. The Pomona team worked to improve their gallium arsenide solar array and even repainted their car a bright orange!

The team from Michigan traveled to Australia in two stages. Seven of the fourteen members flew over in early October to survey the route and begin practice on the road. The other seven team members arrived later, just six days before the race. This was a common procedure among the teams, and as starting day approached, the roads around Darwin became testing grounds for these space-age autos.

On November 5, with six days remaining, Susan Fancy took the Michigan team out to simulate the first day of racing. They started driving at 8:00 AM and drove until 5:00 PM. Pleased with the outcome of the simulation, Fancy felt confident about the Sunrunner's performance. The car had covered 354 miles

(570 kms), farther than expected. Apparently, the greatest difficulty was removing the dead animals which litter the Stuart Highway. They also had to scare away animals that stood in the road, such as dingos, wild horses, cattle and lizards.

"We saw them all," Fancy recalled. "The cattle are fun. They're not really impressed by cars, so you drive up, stop, and then yell and make faces at them until they leave."

The night after the practice run, the Michigan team stayed at a small hotel/restaurant/pub/grocery store/gas station/post office in a place called Daly Waters, about 310 miles (500 km) south of Darwin. The walls were covered with currency from around the world, as well as pictures, posters, police badges (including one they brought from the Ann Arbor Police Department), Rotary club flags, and Outback souvenirs such as turtle shells and snakeskins. Fancy said she expected to see Crocodile Dundee walk in at any moment.

"We had one of the best dinners there that we've had during our entire stay in Australia," Fancy said. "It is what the Aussies call a half-and-half, which is half Barramundi fish and half buffalo steak." Just before leaving the next morning, the team placed a University of Michigan seal (with their signatures) on the back door.

The Michigan team finished up their practice driving on November 7. By the time they returned to Darwin, the place was swarming with people. Hotels and restaurants were jammed as people were coming to watch from all over the world. Rental cars were scarce. Media personnel who had not made prior arrangements were trying to negotiate rides and rent dune-buggies— anything to follow the race.

Pre-race excitement was mounting, and rumors about the competitors were flying. The U.S. teams were confident, but not over-confident. They were aware of the stiff competition. Professional solar car racing teams from many countries were in this race, some from multi-billion dollar corporations such as Honda. Some had years of experience, such as the the team from the Swiss Engineering University of Biel. They had raced in the European Tour de Sol since 1985 and had finished third in the 1987 World Solar Challenge. The 1990 Australian race would be quite a contest!

The international flavor made this race unique. With everyone speaking different languages and waving different flags, the Australian

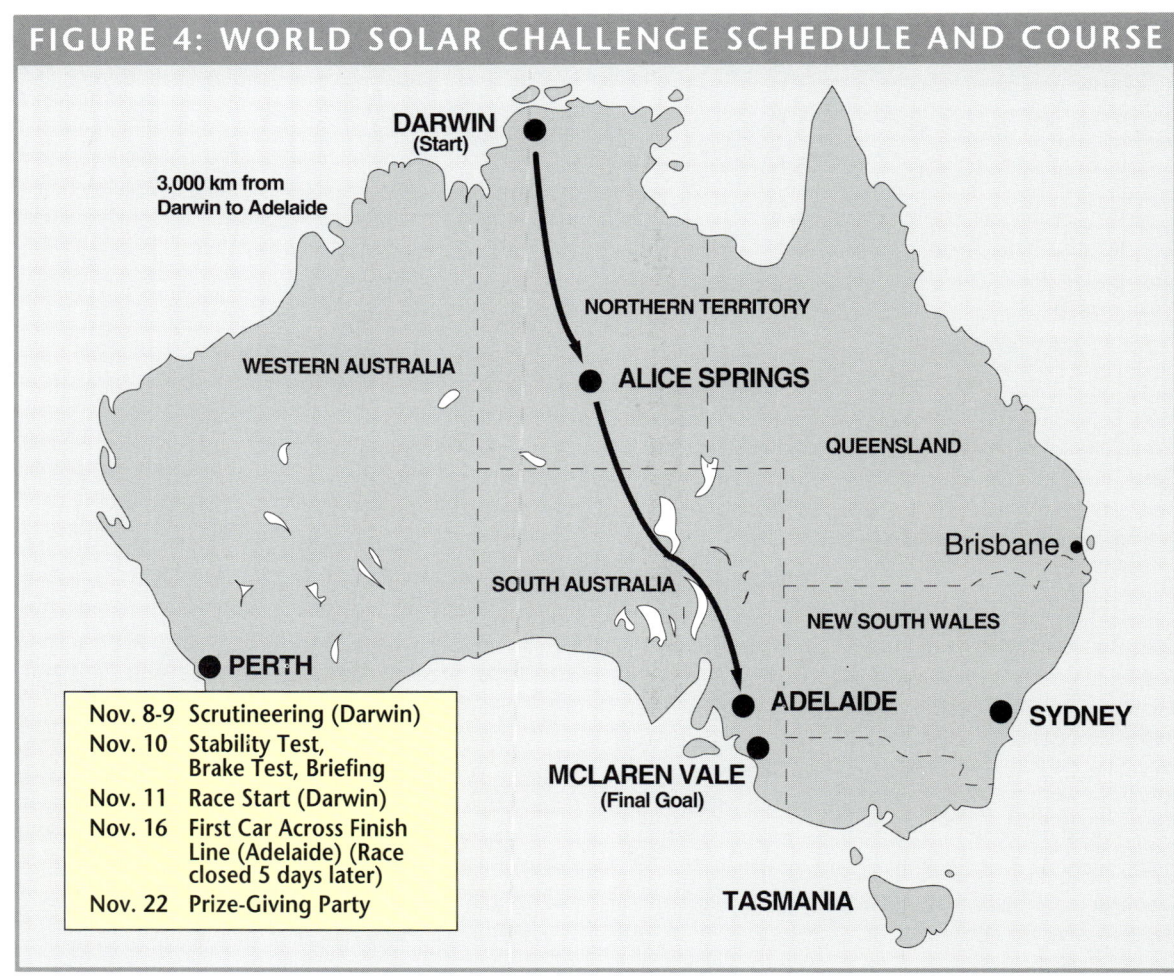

FIGURE 4: WORLD SOLAR CHALLENGE SCHEDULE AND COURSE

3,000 km from Darwin to Adelaide

DARWIN (Start)

NORTHERN TERRITORY

WESTERN AUSTRALIA

ALICE SPRINGS

QUEENSLAND

SOUTH AUSTRALIA

Brisbane

NEW SOUTH WALES

PERTH

ADELAIDE

SYDNEY

MCLAREN VALE (Final Goal)

TASMANIA

Nov. 8-9	Scrutineering (Darwin)
Nov. 10	Stability Test, Brake Test, Briefing
Nov. 11	Race Start (Darwin)
Nov. 16	First Car Across Finish Line (Adelaide) (Race closed 5 days later)
Nov. 22	Prize-Giving Party

TABLE 4: WORLD SOLAR CHALLENGE ENTRY LIST

NO.	TEAM	COUNTRY	NO.	TEAM	COUNTRY
1	Honda R&D, Ltd.	Japan	21	Helio Det 1	Germany
2	Mr. Hirotaka Oyabu	Japan	22	Star Micronics Pty., Ltd.	Australia
3	Graham Davies-Smith	Australia	23	Grundfos Solvogn Denmark	Denmark
4	State of Hawaii-Business &		24	Stanley A. Meyer	Australia
	Economic Development Dept.	USA	25	California State Polytechnic	
5	Semiconductor Energy Lab. (SEL)	Japan		University, Pomona	USA
6	HOXAN Corporation	Japan	26	Mr. Hajime Yamawaki	Japan
7	Delta Solar Team, Inc.	Canada	27	Rendev Solar Team (Mark Jansen)	Australia
8	Dripstone High School	Australia	28	Queen's University, Kingston	Canada
9	Team Barossa	Australia	29	Waseda University	Japan
10	University of Maryland	USA	30	Australian Energy Research Lab	Australia
11	Morphett Vale High School	Australia	31	University of Oklahoma	USA
12	Monash University	Australia	33	Crowder College	USA
14	Mr. Dimitri Lajovic	Australia	35	University of Michigan	USA
15	Northern Territory University	Australia	77	Kyocera-Kitami I.T.	Japan
16	Mr. Phil Farrand	England	83	AISOL	Japan
17	Simon Company, Ltd.	Japan	92	Mr. Michiro Eguchi	Japan
18	Annesley College	Australia	100	Ingenieurschule Biel	Switzerland
19	California State Univ., Los Angeles	USA	101	Mr. Nobuaki Hosokawa	Japan
20	Western Washington University	USA	898	Mr. Stewart Lister	New Zealand

contest lived up to its name, the World Solar Challenge. In this global competition, teams from the U.S. were surprised at how much their competitors knew about SUNRAYCE. They figured the scouting information must have been floating quite freely. Teams from the U.S. felt stronger knowing they were respected as tough competition, especially since they were university students in a field of professional racers. They were proud to represent their schools and their country.

For the most part, SUNRAYCE teams were well-prepared because of their recent racing experience in the States. But the American students knew this event would be even more challenging. The Stuart Highway stretched over 1,870 miles (3,000 km) across the desert Outback to Adelaide. The terrain was flatter and traffic would be minimal, but the distance was 220 miles (354 km) farther than the SUNRAYCE route. This trip also required more planning for the journey itself, since they would not find many conveniences along the way. Service stations, restaurants and hotels are not to be found on every street corner— mainly because street corners do not exist in the Outback! Teams had to be prepared to withstand intense heat and sun and to provide for food, water, and shelter. They had to be ready for any emergency or breakdown that might occur.

The format for the World Solar Challenge is quite different from SUNRAYCE. Racers start at 8 AM and race as far as they can until 5:30 PM. Then they simply stop, put a mark on the road, and pull over to camp for the night. The next morning they start from that spot to begin another day of racing. This sunlit vigil, racing during the day and camping under the stars at night, continues until they cross the finish line in Adelaide. The faster cars reach the finish in five or six days, averaging 40 mph (65 kph). Others might take a week or more to finally reach Adelaide. As this sun-driven procession proceeds across the continent they stretch out for miles. Separated yet bound together by the common desire to prove that their cars can go so far on so little energy.

On November 9 and 10 the cars were brought together for scrutineering and qualifying. The 36 racing teams represented nine different nationalities. There were 11 teams from Australia, 11 from Japan, eight from the U.S., two from Canada, and one each from New Zealand, England, Germany, Denmark, and Switzerland. What an impressive assemblage of vehicles and drivers.

At this point, the drama really began. The preparations were over, and it was time to perform. Each solar car was tested to make sure it complied with race rules. Speed trials the day before the race determined starting positions for all the teams.

The Crowder College team, fifth place winners of SUNRAYCE, arrived in Australia full of confidence. Art Boyt, the faculty advisor, was among those who had raced here three years ago. The Crowder car had finished eighth in that competition. The minute the 1987 race was over, Boyt began considering new ideas for a car that would perform well in the Outback. Now his team was ready for a second try at being the fastest solar car in the

Above: Cal Poly Pomona's newly-painted "Solar Flair."

Left: What makes the World Solar Challenge take on a special character is the wide variety of competitors. There are teams backed by large corporations as well as single individuals who build their cars themselves. Shown left is Dimitri Lajovic's homemade "Allarus," a plastic-covered, two-wheel motorized bike which pulled a solar trailer. He was nicknamed "Darth Vader."

Below: Sponsored by the Semiconducter Energy Laboratory (SEL) of Japan, the "Southern Cross II" used amorphous silicon solar cells, the same type found in solar calculators.

Above: There were several Japanese teams at the World Solar Challenge, including Hoxan's "Phoebus III."

Left The "Spirit of Biel" another pre-race favorite, from Switzerland.

Below: The heavily-favored solar car built by Honda. It was named "Dream" after their first motorcycle and was clocked at 59 mph during qualifying trials.

world. The design of Crowder's two-person vehicle, the Star II, was actually better accommodated to the Australian format than SUNRAYCE.

Crowder's solar car project was small compared to some of the giant corporations they were about to compete with. What they lacked in budget, however, they made up for in spirit and determination. Team leader Steve Tipton believes no one should be afraid to go ahead with a project just because someone else has more money. According to Tipton, Crowder's car was put together with a combination of relatively ordinary parts, but it was built with extraordinary ingenuity.

"Many of us spent 60 hours a week, sometimes with full classes," says Tipton. "Once you start you can't bear to see someone else take over because you helped pioneer that project."

Boyt reflected on his feelings with this return trip Down Under. "We are one of only about 60 cars of this type in the world. We are in a competition against the best of them....in a rather exotic setting, or at least in an exotic circumstance." Boyt refers to this group as an "elite bunch of scientists." He is immensely proud to be among those who blazed the frontier with cars that glide along silently on sun-power from above. And doing this for a couple thousand miles is no small accomplishment.

"Since the prize is only a trophy, we are not in it for the money," Boyt continued. "It's more for bringing the technology, the people and the resources together. He compares this

stage of development for solar cars with the Model T, as both types of vehicles cruise along at around 35 mph (57 kph). Boyt calls it "cutting edge of a new era in transportation.....learning how to push solar electric power to the extreme, and pushing technology to be competitive." According to him, "That's how progress is made."

The scrutineering in Darwin was two-phase. In the first stage, officials checked each car's compliance with safety standards, battery size, weight and vehicle dimensions. By 11 PM on Friday, November 9 all 36 solar cars had passed. The second stage included testing for stability, braking, and top speed to determine pole positions. On Saturday morning each team was required to report to the Hidden Valley race track just outside of town. One by one, the cars lined up to drive down the straightaway. As they drove, each car's stability was tested by having them pass a road train driving in the opposite direction at 65 mph (105 kph). Road trains are huge trailer trucks (three trailers long) that frequent the Stuart Highway. Barreling along at high speeds, these road trains create quite a wake. Each solar car had to prove that it could drive by without being blown off the road. Once past the road train, each car's top speed was measured by a radar gun.

Solar Star, a German-built car financed by an Australian electronics company, won pole position with a recorded speed of 64 mph (103 kph). In second place was the Spirit of Biel from

Each team had to prove that their car could drive by a three-trailer "road train" travelling at 60 mph without being blown off the road. Above: The Japanese solar car sponsored by CSK Simon Co. takes the road train test.

Left: Maryland team member Maureen Williams holds onto the door of the road train.

It was a cloudy, rainy morning for the start of the World Solar Challenge. This photo was taken minutes before the start. Sitting in the pole position (Above: left, front) is the "Solar Star" sponsored by Star Micronics and driven by Michael Trykowski. On the right is the "Spirit of Biel" from Switzerland.

Switzerland with a speed of 63 mph (101 kph). Just behind these two cars from Europe were two Japanese entries: Honda's Dream and Kyocera's Blue Eagle. They were in a tie for third and fourth place, both recording speeds of 59 mph (94 kph). Kyocera is one of Japan's leading photovoltaic solar cell companies.

Close behind was the Pride of Maryland and Cal State L.A.'s Solar Eagle, clocked at 58 and 57 mph (93 and 92 kph) respectively. The other four SUNRAYCE teams were not far behind. The six U.S. teams placed in the top 14 among the world's fastest solar cars.

Final scrutineering was over by Saturday afternoon. Now it was time to race. Teams held final strategy meetings to prepare for Sunday's 8 AM start. The World Solar Challenge would start in front of the Beaufort Hotel in Darwin, overlooking the Indian Ocean. That evening, there was a beautiful red sunset over the water. Soon the earth's rotation would bring the sun back bright as ever to power the cars on toward Adelaide.

A brilliant sun is not what teams woke up to, however. The night had brought rain. By 6 AM it was raining hard in Darwin. Satellite photos showed the storm just over the city, and forecasters predicted the rain would stop by 8 o'clock. Tholstrup postponed the start of the race one hour. Fortunately, the rain did stop. What could have been a gloomy beginning turned into a satisfactory one. Gray skies failed to dampen the spirits of the competitors or the spectators. They were ready for the World Solar Challenge.

This race was definitely different from SUNRAYCE. Not a race solely for university students, this competition included a field of corporate giants, environmentally-conscious businesses, colleges, high schools, and adventurous individuals. Some had million-dollar budgets, while others had minimal funds from their own pockets. The Honda team, for example, had plenty of resources. Their group had 18 professional engineers working on the project. Detlef Schmitz was a startling contrast. This German entrepreneur had built his solar car by himself with old motorcycle parts. One week before the race, he carefully packed it all up in three suitcases and flew it to Australia. It was quite a sight to see him reassemble his car just hours before the start. Here in Darwin the "suitcase man" lined up alongside the huge Honda crew.

Whether teams represented schools, corporations, or nations, they all shared a common purpose. Collectively, they demonstrated that energy concerns are everyone's concerns. Conservation of the earth's resources is an international goal which knows no real boundaries. After all, we populate the same world and breathe the same air.

The World Solar Challenge started at 9 AM on Sunday, November 10. Immediately, the cars jockeyed for position. Teams knew that a strong showing on the first day could put a team hours ahead of competitors. In this race against time, even minutes were critical. From the very beginning, certain cars demonstrated their ability to pull ahead.

As the Hoxan team pulls into a press stop along the Stuart Highway, team members lift off the canopy so a new driver can get in.

Michigan's Sunrunner had started off in tenth place but was leading the pack by the time they reached the city limits. Hoxan began in seventh position and moved up to the second spot. Crowder's Star II had an impressive start by maneuvering from twelfth place to third. Teams found out later that some of the early leaders had gotten caught in city traffic and could not maintain their positions out front. Others, like the Spirit of Biel, experienced early breakdowns and had to stop for repairs.

The unexpected rain and cloudy weather wreaked havoc on team racing strategies. Those who lacked good meteorological data were at a distinct disadvantage. For example, the Japanese Honda team was unaware of the weather forecast the night before the start of the race. They reduced the size of the Dream's battery pack to make the car lighter. Being lightweight with less battery power was a good strategy for sunny days but not for cloudy skies. With only little storage (1.9 kilowatt hours), the Honda team was forced to stop early because of dead batteries. Team leader Takahiro Iwata sighed as they stopped to camp. "It was as if the gods were against us today," he said in dismay.

The cloudy weather also caught the Maryland team off guard, but in a much different way. When they saw the early morning rain, they changed the sprocket on the Pride's drive wheel. The smaller sprocket would conserve energy while they drove in the rain. When the rain stopped and the weather cleared up, the low gear was a mistake. Instead of cruising at 45 mph (70 kph) to keep pace with competitors, the Pride had to settle for 30 mph (48 kph).

Eventually, they stopped to change the gear sprocket for a larger one, but they were already several hours behind the other teams. More accurate weather data would have helped the Maryland team plan accordingly and could have prevented the loss of valuable racing time.

Despite the cloudy skies, the leading cars were making excellent progress out on the road. About 106 miles (170 km) south of Darwin the drivers approached one of the steepest hills of the route, the Hayes Creek Grade. Western Washington's powerful Viking XX arrived first, climbing with ease. Honda, Michigan, and Biel followed and drove up the hill with no apparent problems. Hoxan's Phoebus III, following close behind in fifth place, started up in high gear. But when the driver downshifted, the derailleur got stuck, and the car stalled in the middle of the road.

A tense moment followed as Crowder came up right behind the Hoxan car. Blinded to oncoming traffic by a curve in the road, driver Steve Tipton decided to pass the Phoebus rather than having the Star II get stuck behind Hoxan's car.

Tipton was lucky there was no oncoming traffic. Crowder passed safely and moved into fifth place in the race. Hoxan eventually shifted their derailleur by hand and made it up the hill. To make a bad day worse, the Phoebus III's motor overheated in the process. The Hoxan team had to make a total motor replacement, the first of two they would have to make during the course of the race.

The first press stop for the World Solar Challenge was in the town of Katherine, about 218 miles (350 km) south of Darwin. WWU's Viking arrived first. The Spirit of Biel was right behind, pulling in seconds later. As several other cars arrived, they learned that some of the cars behind them had been caught in a drenching rainstorm. With zero power and no visibility, those cars had to struggle to keep going. Teams which had sprinted ahead toward better weather had chosen a better strategy for day one.

As in the 1987 World Solar Challenge, it was evident by the end of the first day which team would most likely win the race. Three years ago, the GM Sunraycer was several hours ahead of the other cars by the end of the first day's driving. That car won the 1987 race handily. In the 1990 event, the Spirit of Biel showed promise of victory early on. This car drove the farthest distance on the least amount of energy. After driving just one day, it was 25 miles (40 km) ahead of the second-place car, Michigan's Sunrunner.

In this race, the Spirit of Biel even outdistanced the Sunraycer's previous record, traveling 4 miles (6 km) farther than they had in 1987 (527 vs 521 kilometers). By the end of day three, the Biel team had outdistanced the Sunraycer's record by 24 miles (39 km). This was clearly the team to beat in 1990.

No other car in the race was as fast or efficient as the Spirit of Biel. At the end of the first day, the Spirit had 40 percent of its battery power left. By then, most other cars had worn down their batteries completely. The Viking XX had no battery power to spare by late afternoon and dropped from first to third place as they were forced to slow down. Honda's Dream had to stop early for lack of power, settling unhappily into fourth place. The Sunrunner's batteries were low, but the team was able to secure a second-place standing.

As teams set up camp for the night along the highway, they wondered how other cars had fared on day one. The U.S. teams missed the comraderie of finishing up at a common stopping point as they had done in SUN-RAYCE. In the Australian contest there was little opportunity to hear about other teams' experiences. Here, it was not until a scout from another group came by that they had news of competitors' performance on the road. The first evening, Michigan was surprised to learn that Western Washington had camped out just 9 miles (15 km) behind them and that Crowder was just 28 miles (45 km) behind WWU.

On day two the world was a brighter place as the sun poured down in all its glory. The Honda car benefitted most from the change in weather conditions. Being the lightest car, it took off sprightly under full sunlight. By mid-day they passed Western Washington and Michigan to take over second place, however, they couldn't close on the Biel team. With its powerful solar array, the Spirit of Biel was still able to outpace all the other cars. By the end of the second day they had travelled 675 miles (1087 km), 108 miles (173 km) farther than Honda.

With its bright colors glistening across the Outback, the Spirit of Biel made quite an impression as it sped quietly but steadily along the Stuart Highway.

With two days of driving behind them, most teams settled into the routine of the race. Because they were so spread out, it was rare for different crews to see each other. The intense heat and seemingly endless desert made each day seem like the next. Without the constant vigil they kept on their cars' performance, teams might have yielded to boredom. Michigan driver Paula Finnegan found herself singing "A White

By the end of the first day of racing, the Swiss Biel team had driven over 20 miles farther than anyone else. The relaxed feeling at their camp made it seem as if they were going to win.

World Solar Challenge

The format for the World Solar Challenge is different from the GM SUNRAYCE USA in that the solar cars are not grouped together at a common overnight stopping location.

In the World Solar Challenge, the teams start racing at 8:00 am each morning and drive as far as they can. At 5:30 pm each team must stop, put a mark on the road, and pull over to camp. In the morning, they must start where they left off.

The first team to cross the continent to Adelaide is the winner. Racing this way, the teams get separated by miles as they stretch up and down the highway.

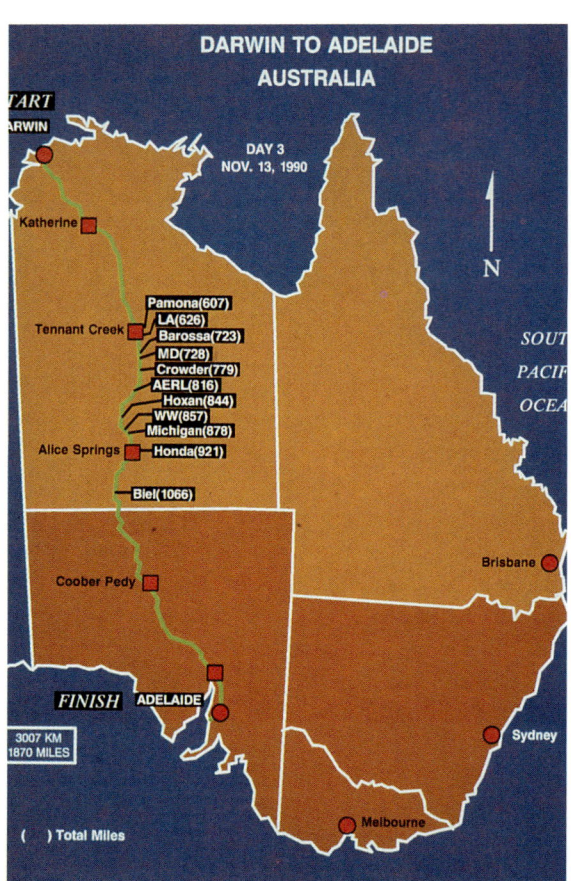

The Honda team (left) camping at the end of the first day. Notice the floor they have to help keep their car immaculate.

The University of Michigan team stops at the end of their fourth day of racing to set up camp (above) and makes final checks (left) to ensure their car remains in top racing condition.

Because there are few service stations or auto parts stores in the Outback, each team had to be prepared to cope with any emergency or breakdown. Many, such as the Maryland team (right), brought a trailer truck filled with supplies, tools and even welding equipment. No matter how prepared a team could get, however, a team member always had to be prepared to use his/her head (bottom right).

Below: The Maryland team holds up their car's solar array to catch some extra sunlight just before starting out for another day of racing.

Christmas," while her teammate David Noles tuned up with Bob Dylan songs.

Teams looked forward to the evening campouts where they exchanged jokes and stories. Some teams had brought along a dedicated cook to prepare dinner for the race-weary crews. Relaxing with a plate of spaghetti and meatballs made for a pleasant day's end. If they were lucky, they might even catch a lightning show from an approaching thunderstorm. Early on, they discovered that sunsets in the Outback are magnificent. Then, the stars would come out with spectacular brilliance. So far from civilization, it seemed as if an outstretched arm could touch them. The racers themselves provided the entertainment for each day on the road, but they appreciated being spectators of mother nature's wonders at night.

With the Biel and Honda teams so far out front, the race for third place captured most of the attention after day two. Michigan, Hoxan, and Western Washington exchanged places several times as they vied for position. By day four they were all within 19 miles (30 km) of each other. It was anyone's guess which team might end up in the hotly-contested third place. When the Phoebus III burned out its second motor and the Viking XX got caught in strong crosswinds, Michigan held onto the number three spot. The Hoxan team never gave the Michigan

team a chance to rest, though. They seemed to race almost neck-and-neck up to the finish line.

At 1:15 PM on Friday, November 16 the Spirit of Biel arrived at the finish line in Adelaide. The team had traveled the 1,870-mile distance (3,007 km) in 46 hours at an average speed of 40.5 mph (65 kph), just missing the Sunraycer's record. Three years earlier the GM car had made the trip in just under 45 hours with an average speed of 41.7 mph (66.9 kph). Biel missed the record because clouds and a strong crosswind on day four slowed their progress.

Although the race was over for one team, 36 others were still on the highway. The World Solar Challenge requires that competitors drive the entire route as fast as possible. With each passing day, the distance between the solar cars changed until many were literally days apart on the road. Interested spectators had to keep watch for several days to find out which teams had made it all the way to Adelaide.

The next day, Honda's Dream pulled into the winner's circle. In accordance with Japanese tradition, the team proceeded to throw their drivers into the air and catch them. They repeated this scene several times. Then, they tossed team leader Takahiro Iwata into a nearby lake as part of their celebration. The Honda crew was thrilled to capture second place.

The "Spirit of Biel" crosses the finish line to win the 1990 World Solar Challenge.

The Western Washington team performed well in the World Solar Challenge, finishing fifth overall. Here the team is shown lifting their car up to turn it around.

Meanwhile, Michigan and Hoxan were still battling it out for third place. The two cars were in sight of each other just outside of Adelaide when the Sunrunner had a flat tire. The Michigan team made its tire change at lightning's speed, yelling at each other to hurry as the Hoxan car pulled up beside them. The Sunrunner zoomed off with the Phoebus III right behind. Using every ounce of the car's energy, the Michigan team was determined to beat Hoxan to the finish line.

Two hours after Honda's Dream, the Sunrunner raced under the checkered flag. The Michigan team made it just six minutes ahead of the Hoxan car, taking third place overall. The students realized they had captured their spot in the winner's circle by the skin of their teeth! A throng of reporters descended upon them, while champagne corks popped everywhere. While congratulating Biel and Honda, they heard about the Japanese tradition. A few minutes later, Susan Fancy ended up in the lake, tossed in by her triumphant team. She did not seem to mind at all, as she came up smiling.

These three teams representing three different continents were soon exchanging handshakes, hugs, and stories. After they decided to trade T-shirts with each other it was difficult to tell who was from where. Reporters had a tough time, but the racers were too excited to notice.

One hour later, at 4:07 PM, the Viking XX crossed the finish line. The team from Western Washington had done exceptionally well but experienced stability problems with the crosswinds on the Stuart Highway. The Viking's large solar panel, angled to catch the sun's rays, also caught the wind. Drivers learned to proceed cautiously as they were buffeted by strong gusty winds across the

Outback. By the fourth day, they assumed a rather conservative strategy for racing even though their powerful array had plenty of energy for faster driving. They were delighted with their fifth place finish and joined the other American teams in celebrating their victory.

While this celebration was going on, Crowder and Maryland were still in a tight race for seventh place. A bit farther back the other U.S. teams, Cal State L.A. and Pomona, were vying for the tenth spot. These teams were rather surprised to end up challenging each other so closely in this field of 36 competitors.

Crowder's Star II had started well in the race and thought they had a secure hold on seventh place. After all, they had not even had a glimpse of their competitors from Maryland since day one. Then, on day four of the race, the Pride astonished everyone by coming up from behind. The Maryland car covered 338 miles (544 km) on that day to catch up and pass the Star II, moving 14 miles (22 km) ahead of the Missouri team.

When this happened, Art Boyt was amazed at his team's resilience. The Crowder students had learned from their SUNRAYCE experience that races can be won or lost by mere minutes. The Star II had lost fourth place in the U.S. race by less than three minutes. In Australia, they refused to give up. Determined to do their best, the Crowder team rallied to keep going full speed ahead.

By the seventh day the Crowder team was within 75 miles (120 km) of Adelaide. Suddenly, the Australian Team Barossa came from nowhere and passed them. Unwilling to lose their standing in eighth place, the Crowder driver floored the accelerator to drive side-by-side with Team Barossa. By day's end the two teams were so close that they shared the same evening campsite.

On the morning of November 18, Team Barossa pulled in front of the Star II. Traffic in Adelaide made it impossible for Steve Tipton to pass. The Crowder team could not help feeling somewhat glum, but the beautiful rolling countryside lifted their spirits a bit. Just outside of McLaren Vale, the site of the World Solar Challenge finish line, was a very steep hill. As the Star II made its way up, the team spotted the Team Barossa car stalled out on the incline. With bolstered feelings, Crowder raced on to pass the other car. Crowder's Star II made it to the finish line only 16 minutes in front of the Australian team. They had captured eighth place after all and were ecstatic!

Beating a competitor by a close margin provides a thrill equal to winning. Teams from Maryland, Western Washington, and Michigan were on hand to congratulate the Crowder students. Of course, Art Boyt got dunked in the lake as part of the celebration. Emerging wet but happy, Boyt blurted out with a smile, "A week without a shower and now this!"

Later that day Cal State L.A. and Pomona also arrived in Adelaide. These two teams were in tenth and eleventh place after a breathtakingly close race. Ironically, these schools are arch rivals in the States, and here they were racing neck-and-neck an ocean away!

As they neared the finish, Pomona was in the lead. But the Solar Flair's chain came off repeatedly because it was so worn down. Cal State's Solar Eagle had remained on their tail all day, making the Pomona crew incredibly nervous. As the cars approached the hill outside McLaren Vale, the team from Cal State saw their chance. The Solar Flair's chain came off once again, and the Eagle soared past. The team from L.A. was elated. In fact, faculty leader Ray Landis claims he would have had to swim all the way back to Los Angeles if Pomona had beaten his team!

The World Solar Challenge awards banquet was held on Thursday, November 22. Back in the United States, it was Thanksgiving Day 1990. The victory celebration took place at the McLaren Vale Estate. An old winery on the grounds had been renovated and remodeled as

The World Solar Challenge finished at McLaren Vale, located in the heart of Australia's most scenic wine country. The "Spirit of Biel's" winning time to finish the 1,870 mile course was 46 hours, 8 minutes (average 40.7 mph), 1 hour and 14 minutes behind "Sunraycer's" record established in 1987 (average speed 41.7 mph). Biel would have beaten the record except for strong cross winds between Coober Pedy and Port Augusta.

The media swarms around the second place Honda car just after it crossed the finish line almost a day behind the "Spirit of Biel."

a resort hotel, and this is where the teams saluted each other. Hundreds of people attended the evening event. As he surveyed the crowd, race director Hans Tholstrup was obviously pleased.

Howard Wilson, affectionately known as the grandfather of solar car racing, was on hand to present the first place award. In 1987, Wilson was the leader of GM's Sunraycer team, so it was only fitting that he bestow the honors on the winning team of the 1990 event. Wilson handed the victory trophy, a sparkling World Solar Cup, to Biel team members Fredy Sidler and René Jeanneret. As Wilson praised the team's car, the mighty Spirit of Biel, Sidler proudly held up the trophy and announced that his team would return to defend the championship in 1993. The audience responded with a standing ovation for this impressive team from Switzerland.

Takahiro Iwata accepted the second-place trophy for the Honda team. He thanked the organizers for providing such a challenging learning experience and congratulated the Biel team for their excellent performance. Iwata had special praise for the enthusiastic group of students from Michigan. Their car, the bright yellow Sunrunner, had stayed on the Dream's tail throughout the race. He noted that the Michigan team never gave the Japanese team a chance to rest.

Accepting the third place trophy for the Michigan team, Susan Fancy was overcome with emotion. Extremely proud of her dedicated team and the iron-clad reliability of the Sunrunner, Fancy thanked the University of Michigan and General Motors for making this historical moment happen. She was well-aware of the significance of victory for a university team in this international event. What she had only dreamed of had finally become reality.

All six U.S. teams performed well in the 1990 World Solar Challenge. Finishing in the top eleven spots, their performance showed that aspiring scientists and engineers from America's universities have what it takes to compete with the world's best.

In his closing remarks, Tholstrup called the World Solar Challenge the most important race in the world. The event had captured the attention of millions to show that there are good clean solutions to today's energy problems. The modern-day "brain sport" asks scientists and engineers to challenge each other with concepts and technologies slightly ahead of their time. As he congratulated the teams, he called them the "believers and visionaries who carry the torch" and told them to keep the spirit alive.

The Sunrunner team celebrates after finishing in third place.

TABLE 5: WORLD SOLAR CHALLENGE FINAL STANDINGS

POSITION	TEAM NAME	TOTAL DISTANCE(km)	TOTAL TIME (hrs)	AVERAGE SPEED mph	kph
1	Biel	3007	46.131	41	65
2	Honda	3007	54.997	34	55
3	Michigan	3007	57.247	33	53
4	Hoxan	3007	57.347	33	53
5	W. Washington	3007	58.497	32	51
6	AERL	3007	59.897	31	50
7	Maryland	3007	60.714	31	50
8	Crowder	3007	62.964	30	48
9	Barossa	3007	63.285	30	48
10	Calif. State, LA	3007	67.764	28	44
11	Pomona	3007	68.031	28	44
12	N.T. Univ.	3007	69.614	27	43
13	Monash Univ.	3007	69.814	27	43
14	Kyocera	3007	71.381	26	42
15	Trykowski	3007	80.064	23	38
16	Simon	3007	90.941	21	33
17	Lajovic	3007	94.714	20	32
18	Hawaii H.S.	3007	96.206	20	31
19	Dripstone H.S.	3007	96.574	19	31
20	Annesley	2974*	96.831	19	31
21	Sofix	2938*	96.831	19	30
22	Waseda	2915*	96.831	19	30
23	Stewart Lister	2842*	96.831	18	29
24	Queens Univ.	2494*	96.831	16	26
25	AISOL	2456*	96.831	16	25
26	Yamawaki	2110*	96.831	14	22
27	Barclay	2071	96.831	13	21
28	SEL	1996	96.831	13	21
29	Hekio Det	1961	96.831	13	20
30	Solar Japan	1900	96.831	12	19
31	Denmark**	2025			
32	Morphett H.S.	718	Retired		
33	England	320	Retired		
34	Hosokawa	124	Retired		
35	Mark Jensen	102	Retired		
36	Univ. of Oklahoma	5	Retired		

*These cars continued to Adelaide on solar power after the official finish of the race.
** Destroyed by a "willy nilly" (mini-tornado).

After finishing in seventh place, the University of Maryland had their own private victory celebration. The highlight came when team members grabbed team leader Larry Long, carried him down to the lake. and ceremoniously threw him in!

The Crowder team begins their celebration (left) after finishing in eighth place, less than two hours behind Maryland. Ecstatic at their accomplishment, the team lifts their solar car up (below) in triumphant unison. In this race, everyone is a winner.

VII. The Silent Revolution

The sport of sunracing is a competitive blend of human skill and technological ingenuity. Using cars that demonstrate alternative energy sources, sunracing lifts the sport of auto racing to new levels of sophistication. Instead of sheer speed and chilling nerve, sunracing involves intricate strategies based on changing variables. Optimization and efficiency are the key ingredients.

The object of solar car racing is NOT to see who can drive the fastest at death-defying speeds. Instead, the object is to determine who best navigates a solar car over a long distance while collecting sunlight for fuel. At the same time, this sport demonstrates the benefits of solar energy. Sunracing shows how we can conserve resources and protect the environment without sacrificing mobility. Solar car racing poses new and refreshing challenges while advancing electric vehicle technology. It even provides opportunities for good, clean fun!

One reason for the rather slow acceptance of solar electric technology is the lack of general knowledge about how it works. When asked about photovoltaics, most people will respond with a blank stare. Sunracing has proven to be a successful means of increasing public awareness of photovoltaic technology. Solar car races have generated increased interest and understanding of solar electricity, an important first step toward greater use of this alternative energy source.

University students in GM SUNRAYCE USA reaped tremendous benefits as participants in solar car projects. Designing, building, and racing solar cars provided real-life situations where students could apply academic learning. The race gave students a chance to take part in a large multi-disciplinary project which required collaboration and cooperation. Teamwork served as an opportunity to develop both professional and interpersonal skills.

The solar cars built by SUNRAYCE teams serve another purpose as well. They attract attention to university and college engineering departments. Some schools have used their solar cars as recruitment tools, hoping to entice greater numbers of high school students to pursue careers in science and engineering.

There are close to 300 million cars in the world today.

This megawatt size photovoltaic solar plant provides electricity to the utility grid in California.

Competitions motivate people to excel. Sunracing is no different. When Hans Tholstrup created the World Solar Challenge he sensed that the world needed a race to get the best scientists and engineers together. Tholstrup says, "When I drive behind a better driver in a car race, I learn to be just as good, sometimes better. When someone jumps over a hurdle and sees another person jump higher, they get motivated and jump even higher; then we all get higher." The same message can be applied to solar car racing. We all learn so much.

In a sense, solar car races are R&D test beds for new advanced technologies that eventually end up in tomorrow's automobiles. The innovation in the race vehicles will eventually help improve electric vehicles for the consumer. These competitions also push automobile companies toward greater efficiency in auto design. Ultimately, the sport of sunracing can help us solve today's energy, transportation, and environmental problems.

We need solutions sooner rather than later. Statistics describing automobile use are staggering. At present, there are over 300 million cars on the world's roads. These cars travel trillions of miles each day and are responsible for producing over one-third of all atmospheric pollution. And, vehicle usage is constantly on the rise. The world's population is increasing and less-developed countries are improving their standard of living to include more auto use.

An illustration of the severity of this problem comes from the 1991 Gulf War. Iraqi soldiers ignited most of Kuwait's oil wells just before they were pushed out by U.S. soldiers. Americans were outraged at the black skies they saw on their TV screens, fearing the extent of the environmental pollution. The smoke covered hundreds of square miles and was so thick it seemed like a nuclear winter in and around Kuwait. At the height of the burning, an estimated three million barrels of oil were going up in smoke each day. Most Americans failed to realize that they burn almost three times that amount every day just by driving cars and trucks. In addition, American drivers burn six times that amount for other energy needs. That's just in the United States. Taken literally, there is a fire raging around the globe– a huge fire that is continually growing.

In time, oil will become a very precious commodity. If it were more valuable, perhaps people would not use it so carelessly. Just imagine using gold to fuel your car. You would stuff the gold into the engine along with a lot of air so it would have oxygen to burn. In doing so, you would destroy both. Your gold would be gone, and the air would be unusable. Americans spend billions of dollars for oil, just to have it go up in smoke. That's a high price to pay for a short ride.

Since we seem "stuck" with fossil fuels, we ought to learn to use the energy more efficiently. If we eke out more miles per gallon of gasoline in our cars, we will use less gas and reduce atmospheric pollution. If we get 40 miles per gallon instead of 20 miles per gallon, we will inject half the amount of pollutants into the air; at 80 miles per gallon, only one-fourth as much. The solar cars described in this book demonstrated that they could be driven over a thousand miles on the equivalent of a single gallon of gasoline.

Will we be driving solar powered cars in the future? Maybe, but not right away. Present-day automobiles are too heavy. Solar racing cars collect approximately one horsepower of solar energy. That is just enough to power a 400-pound vehicle at 40 mph. Today's full-size passenger cars weigh 2,000-4,000 pounds and require at least ten times as much horsepower. The average compact car on the road uses one hundred times as much power.

What we might be driving in the near future are electric vehicles partially powered by

Solar Car Corporation in Florida converts these Ford Festivas into electric cars and uses the solar panels on the roof and hood to give the car extra range. The solar panels also help to extend the life of the batteries.

solar cells. Some manufacturers sell electric commuter cars with solar cells mounted on the roof and/or hood. Whenever these cars are driven or parked in the sun, the cells provide electricity for the batteries. For short driving errands, the car's batteries will have more energy after a 20-minute park outside than when the car was first parked. For cars sitting in traffic, there is a double benefit; the engine is not running (or polluting) and the solar cells are recharging the batteries. When people at work park a car outside all day, the batteries are fully recharged when it's time to go home. The solar cells also extend the life of the batteries, which helps make this type of car more economical to maintain.

Large solar cell arrays could also be mounted on house, garage, or car-port roofs to provide the necessary electricity for electric vehicles. One such system is being planned in California to prepare for a state law that will go into effect in 1998. The law will require two

percent of all cars sold in California to be zero pollution-emitters. The photovoltaic system will be mounted on the roof of a parking lot carport. During the day the PV system will recharge electric vans.

With so much progress the future looks bright. In June 1993 a second Sunrayce will take place with 36 new teams of university students. The route will stretch from Texas up through America's heartland to Minnesota. Later that year, in November, the third World Solar Challenge will take place in Australia. Meanwhile, the Swiss Tour de Sol will be held annually, along with a growing number of other solar and electric car races around the world.

The pioneers who created the sport of sun-racing started a "silent revolution" in transportation. In time, solar and electric vehicle technologies may be applied to most of the cars we drive. That will be a major step toward a cleaner world for us all.

This is an artist's conception of a solar car port used to recharge electric vehicles. The demonstration project is being funded by Southern California Edison and will be located near Los Angeles, California.

The Grand Solar Challenge was held on an ocean beach. Here was the lineup just prior to the start.

The Japanese are very clever at animating some of their solar cars. They had two cars that looked like cats, one that looked like a mouse, and one that looked like a whale.

Toyota's new solar car is lined up in second position just beside the "Spirit of Biel" and in front of the University of Maryland. The Toyota car narrowly beat the "Sprit of Biel" by two minutes.

Grand Solar Challenge

The Grand Solar Challenge was held in Japan in August, 1992. It was the largest, most dazzling solar car rally ever held. With 103 solar cars entered, it boasted a competitive field that included cars built by Honda, Toyota, and Nissan. Some of our Pacific friends are taking this new sport seriously.

Above: Nissan's new solar car.